Reflections
from the Journey of Life

Reflections
from the Journey of Life
Collected Sayings of the Dalai Lama

Previously unpublished sayings
of the Fourteenth Dalai Lama
collected and edited by

Catherine Barry
from speeches and
personal conversations

Translated from the French by
Joseph Rowe

North Atlantic Books
Berkeley, California

Published by
North Atlantic Books
P.O. Box 12327
Berkeley, California 94712

www.northatlanticbooks.com

Cover and book design by Paula Morrison
Printed in the United States of America

Cover art: Four-armed Avalokitesvara. Appliqued thangka from Tibet. The Newark Museum/Art Resource, NY. The four-armed form of Avalokitesvara, Bodhisattva of Mercy, is believed to incarnate in the Dalai Lama.

Originally published in French by Édtions 1, 2001.

Thank you to the French Ministry of Culture for partially funding this publication.

Reflections from the Journey of Life is sponsored by the Society for the Study of Native Arts and Sciences, a nonprofit educational corporation whose goals are to develop an educational and crosscultural perspective linking various scientific, social, and artistic fields; to nurture a holistic view of arts, sciences, humanities, and healing; and to publish and distribute literature on the relationship of mind, body, and nature.

Library of Congress Cataloging-in-Publication Data
Bstan-'dzin-rgya-mtsho, Dalai Lama XIV, 1935–
    Reflections from the journey of life : collected sayings of the Dalai Lama
    / by Catherine Barry.
        p. cm.
    ISBN 1-55643-388-3 (pbk. : alk. paper)
    1. Spiritual life—Buddhism. 2. Conduct of life. 3. Buddhism—Doctrines. I. Title: Collected sayings of the Dalai Lama. II. Barry, Catherine, 1955– Sage paroles du Dalai Lama. English. III. Title.

BQ5670 .B76 2002
294.3'923—dc21   2002022380

            1 2 3 4 5 6 7 8 9 / 06 05 04 03 02

To Benjy

To Tulku Pema Wangyal

As long as space exists,
As long as there are sentient beings,
May I also continue to exist,
So as to relieve the world's suffering
And help other beings to be happy.
                    (From the Bodhisattva Vow)

FOREWORD

This book may be read on several levels.

The sole purpose of these introductory sections is to offer some information about the personality of the Dalai Lama, and to clarify some basic notions for those unfamiliar with Buddhist concepts.

For some, these sections may appear simplistic; for others, unfamiliar and difficult.

But this is not important. The real value of this collection is in the words of the Dalai Lama himself. It is enough to read these words, to understand them, to let them sink in . . . and then to read them again and meditate upon them.

Whether used as a bedside companion, a reference work of timeless wisdom, or as a source of daily guidance and inspiration, one can find in these sayings a response to every mood of mind and soul, at any moment of any day.

TABLE OF CONTENTS

THE DALAI LAMA, APOSTLE OF PEACE

"If I look back, I would have to say that the most beautiful
years of my life were spent in Tibet, when it was still a free
country."
— Tenzin Gyatso, the Fourteenth Dalai Lama

Kundun—*The Presence.*

This is what he is called by his own people.

*But to speak the name "Kundun" aloud now in Tibet can
provoke fear and reprisals—the public invocation of the name
of the country's spiritual guide and temporal leader is a pun-
ishable offense. But his centuries-old guidance in the peaceful
conquest of the mind continues to be effective, and even a policy
of physical and cultural genocide has not succeeded in closing
people's hearts, in its attempts to extinguish their freedom of
expression.*

*Kundun—this is now a name which brings people together
around the world: in India, Europe, the United States, and in
all the other lands of Tibetan exile. Though often separated by
enormous distances from their homeland and from each other,
they are still deeply connected to their roots, outwardly visible
through the ubiquitous wine-colored robes, the same as worn*

by all lamas, from lowest to highest in rank.

He has many other names—Dalai Lama (Ocean of Wisdom) being the best known—but also Power of the Word, Incarnation of the Buddha of Compassion, Keeper of the Faith, and Living Emanation of Divinity.

His role is to show the true way, though his teaching is not always well understood by younger generations more oriented to revolt instead of what appears to them to be passivity. But those who would take up arms forget that Buddhism—and especially he who incarnates its teaching—cannot condone any policy of violence, whatever its motivations or excuses.

He is often and widely praised for his non-violent struggle. This led to the Nobel Peace Prize in 1989, an outward recognition by the international community of a wisdom whose origins are inward, the fruit of many centuries of cultivation.

By his own example and actions, he brings encouragement and hope to those who are discouraged and despairing. He openly offers forgiveness to the invaders of his country, while reminding them and the world that the Tibetan people refuse to forget who they are, refuse to allow their own culture and identity to be trampled into oblivion.

He is a beacon of survival for his people. This survival is also a path which he has been discovering and laying out, little by little, ever since that terrible night of March 17, 1959. Disguised as a soldier, with an old English rifle on his shoulder, he was forced to flee his homeland. He left behind not only the summer palace where he had been living, but the Potala, Lhassa, and Tibet itself, where thirteen generations of his predecessors had lived. Far from being an act of escapism, this was a reluctant, last-minute flight which demanded courage and sacrifice.

A sacrifice indeed: in spite of the advice of many of those closest to him, who had been urging him to flee for years, he had steadfastly refused, until there was no alternative, to leave his people and his country in the ruinous clutches of the Chinese invaders. An indispensable sacrifice as well—his concern was not for his personal survival—but to allow himself as living symbol of Tibetan Buddhism to be murdered or imprisoned and silenced by the Chinese, would have been catastrophic for Tibetans' morale and for the survival of their culture. Because of compassion, love, and his duty as spiritual and governmental leader of his people, he was obliged to take the road of exile. On March 31, 1959, he and his party quietly crossed the border into India.

He is perhaps the last of the Dalai Lamas. If peace and autonomy are someday achieved for Tibet, a separation of religious and political power might well prevail, wherein Tenzin Gyatso could willingly abandon his title. In that case, the cycle of his rebirths as Dalai Lama would come to an end. A simple monk, he would take his place among the other lamas. He himself would prefer this—but not until his people are free of the persecution and misery which now engulf them.

Simply to be in his presence is a blessing for anyone. One can understand why he is regarded as a divine incarnation, whom most Tibetans would risk their lives to meet. Even the toughest mountain nomads kneel before him as seekers of truth, with tears running down their cheeks. They leave him inspired and filled with the very quality they worship in him. They open their hearts, telling him of the terrible oppression they have endured. And many return to Tibet with his encouragement, so that their country may continue to live and not be emptied of its soul. At

present there are only six million Tibetans left in their own country, where seven million Chinese settlers have now been "voluntarily deported" to colonize the land of sages. The invasion
continues to advance, over fifty years later.

Exiled Tibetans now come from all over the planet to hear
Kundun speak, to follow and practice his teachings with him. It
is a unique and wonderful exchange and communion.

The more aware a Westerner is of these people's sufferings
and the power and significance which the Dalai Lama embod-
ies for them, the more one feels the tremendous privilege of being
allowed to spend time with him. Tenzin Gyatso seems to draw
everyone around him into an impressive whirl of energy and
wisdom. His presence is an undistorted mirror in which one can
see and feel that the Way he advocates is indeed possible, and
accessible, for us as well.

The first Dalai Lama was born in 1391 C.E., and the fourteenth was born in 1935 C.E. Six centuries separate the current
incarnation from the first, when the world scarcely knew of
Tibet's existence. Since 1989, the Dalai Lama has become a major
figure in the Western media, one of those rare beings whose role
as peacemaker is universally recognized. He has become a kind
of model for many, this apostle of non-violence with twinkling
eyes and playful wit, who stands alone confronting international
superpowers. His serenity, radiance, and grace seem to evoke a
natural mood of contemplation in all who listen to his words.
The search for inner peace knows no borders. It is nurtured by
courage, determination, and by a serene yet informed will. Thus
we make progress, day by day, in our quest for wisdom. With
Kundun, we can realize this quest.

The Buddhism of the Roof of the World

"The essence of Buddhism is universal. Its meaning is independent of any era or place. On the other hand, the outer trappings of Tibetan Buddhism, such as certain rituals, ceremonies, and initiations which are closely bound to our own culture, may be transformed and adapted to a different cultural context, as Buddhism develops in other countries. How should these changes be put into effect? Only time can answer this question."

— The Fourteenth Dalai Lama

Tibetan Buddhism, more properly known as Vajrayana, is practiced throughout the Himalayas. It is also characterized as a science of spirit.

The word science implies a pragmatic approach, based on one's own experience. As with every scientific experiment, we want to understand the mechanisms at work—the principles behind the teaching—so as to be able to repeat them until they are mastered, intimately integrated into our practice so that it becomes natural and spontaneous. Years, perhaps even lifetimes, may be necessary. Whether the phenomena that result are physical or more subtle and inward, the basic principles are the same. They are based on facts, on our knowledge and understanding of things, and on our own point of view, which is necessarily a subjective one, involving what has produced us and who we are.

This is why the Buddha always urged his disciples to test his

---

words, to verify his teachings for themselves, believing nothing merely because of tradition or attachment to him. He desired that we not be slaves of our own emotions, dependent on the relationships we construct with beings, objects, and concepts— even the concept of the Buddha.

The mind is the axis of this Way. Everything that concerns it, all the factors that influence and change it, must be studied and worked with. For most practitioners, this does not imply any sort of retreat from worldly life. It might appear that those who do retreat, sometimes withdrawing in solitude for dozens of years, have escaped this rule. But this is only an appearance— in reality, they have the same obligation to work on themselves for the benefit of all beings. Just like the rest of us, they follow a teaching which must be applied in every instant of life, leading us to live more and more consciously, and in spiritual communion with the whole cosmos. This involves an application of methods based on a fundamental principle of Buddhism: the mutually interdependent arising and existence of all phenomena and all beings. This also explains why certain solitary adepts whose meditations and practices are based on this principle have been able to develop a sensitivity and perception in which they feel no loneliness, in spite of their extreme physical isolation. This is what gives meaning to monkish seclusion: the elimination of all distractions enables them to experience this fundamental truth in a fullness which gives them spiritual strength ... and, it is said, enables them to perform subtle but real actions affecting this world from which they have temporarily withdrawn on a physical level. Such a possibility can no longer be dismissed as fantasy, for it is now supported by scientific theories of chaos, in which the "butterfly effect" makes it possible to have a planetary situation of forces so exquisitely balanced and interrelated that the beating of a butterfly's wings near the Eiffel Tower may trigger a hurricane in Japan.

But it is above all in relation to ordinary, everyday life that this fundamental teaching of interdependence applies. Spiritual life and everyday life are inseparably linked. One's everyday way of being is both the alchemical crucible and the living proof of how far the disciple has come.

Thus everything that has to do with the mind, our own mind, is related to the totality of living beings, especially other humans and animals. Every one of our acts, thoughts, and words leave imprints upon our surroundings, both visible and invisible. These affect our lives now and to come, and reverberate throughout nature and the universe. Knowledge, skillful means, wisdom, and compassion are the pillars of this teaching. Wisdom destroys ignorance and enables us to understand the illusory nature of phenomena, opening access to supreme Truth and Reality. And this in turn engenders even greater compassion.

Everything depends on the mind, for it creates the totality of our experience in projecting what it is at this moment onto things and beings. The nature of its motivation is crucial and decisive. Through understanding its mechanisms we begin to approach and discover its fundamental nature, which is none other than Buddha-nature itself, the heart of all reality.

The mind is the raw material with which the disciple works. Certain practices will be useful for some, but not always for others, for we must experience the mind directly from our own inner nature in order to understand and to change. The better we understand ourselves, the better we understand others. Self-knowledge also makes us more tolerant by accepting our own *human condition, so that the faults and weaknesses which bind us can be worked upon by our deeper nature, so rich with marvelous gifts which ask only to be revealed. When we truly know ourselves, how can we ever presume to pass judgment on others?*

To live more consciously is to be less enslaved by our emotions, more responsible and truly free. Consciousness requires a mindful observation and awareness which can be either concentrated or relaxed and open. This is described by Buddhist teachings as the indispensable cord which bridles our mind and helps us to master it.

Our own lifetime is a priceless opportunity, according to Buddhism. To be born as a human being, instead of in one of the less favorable of the six realms, is said to be a rare privilege. Every moment of this life is precious.

There are many different ways within Buddhism, but the red thread which unites the vast community of practitioners is this "work" on the mind. And, at least in the beginning, it is very demanding work. Some high Tibetan lamas, such as Dzongsar Khyentse Rinpoche (director of the film La Coupe) say that if beginners were really aware of what being a Buddhist implies, many would drop out.

Indeed, Buddhism should not be regarded as a comfortable way! Just as in a scientific experiment, the seeker has a goal in mind: in this case, to realize one's own awakening and freedom from suffering, so as to help all beings to realize this happiness. Hence it is out of the question to adopt this way in order to escape or deny our problems. With trust in the teacher and teachings which guide and support us, we are both protected and encouraged when having to confront ourselves and others as we really are.

Nor is exoticism a viable motivation, for it cannot bring us happiness. To be attracted to Buddhism because it is exotic is to view it as something which is foreign to our everyday nature. But Buddhism is dedicated to revealing the most intimate truth about oneself. Division has no place here. If someone has true affinity for the Buddhist way, it will be revealed in a sense of wholeness experienced during the early learning stages. If the Dalai Lama and other masters manifest such a positive and cheerful attitude in spite of the horrors they have experienced, and are able to communicate this attitude to others, it is because they are impregnated with these teachings, having practiced them since childhood. This requires a profound commitment for which mere curiosity can never be a sufficient motivation.

Our transformation through work on the mind also implies a true and authentic contact with a master who can guide us and listen to our accounts of our trials and errors. This listening is one of love, acceptance, and recognition, not judgment. This kind of unconditional acceptance and recognition is rare in our Western world, where people experience an incredible lack of self-acceptance and self-confidence. One may already feel a sense of being reborn, just being listened to in this way. This guide is also there to protect our very life in a sense, for self-hatred and guilt are peculiarly Western poisons, which attack life at its source. Such notions are quite strange to most Tibetans. But the deep link that is established between teacher and student goes far beyond these cultural differences, and even the consolation that is offered is in the interest of a deeper transformation.

One of the most striking stories of compassionate withholding of judgment is that of Milarepa, one of the greatest masters of Tibetan Buddhism. Yet before entering the Buddhist way,

Milarepa was the worst sort of villain: a black magician, who used his considerable yogic powers to murder others in vengeance for his mother's death. But his teacher Marpa had compassion for him, and so Milarepa was able to demonstrate how far one can evolve in just one lifetime. His story is one of great hope and encouragement in overcoming the most awesome obstacles.

There are no dogmas or imposed beliefs in Buddhism, including the doctrine of reincarnation. We should not "believe" in what a master tells us if it cannot be verified by our own experience, any more than we should believe in what a scientist tells us if we cannot demonstrate it by experimentation. Whether or not we find the story of transmigration through many lives a useful one, we are still faced with the essential question of what to do with this life here and now.

Progressive self-transformation brings greater balance and peace of mind. We are all subject to certain mental and emotional habits. Meditation, visualization, concentration, and mindfulness can help us to realize this goal of spiritual transformation. If we want a more vigorous and healthy body, we engage in exercise and sports—the same principle applies to the mind, though the means are quite different.

Another fundamental teaching is that of impermanence. Nothing exists in itself, or permanently. Human beings grasp at certain situations and try to establish themselves therein so as to avoid suffering and self-questioning. We hide our dead as quickly as possible, for we are very afraid of any manifestation of impermanence, and what it says about the passing of time and the instability of all that exists in time. We are always thinking about futures which rarely come to pass as we imagine them. We would like to have power over time, over things, and over other beings.

Yet learning to see and accept the fact that all things must change can actually bring us the most profound reassurance, for it brings us into communion with the truth. This concept of impermanence prepares us by evoking our deepest capacity of adaptation.

The gift of forgiveness also flows from this realization. To forgive others for what the suffering they have caused us becomes natural, for we now see clearly the more fundamental truth that it is we ourselves who create our own suffering.

Every religion espouses the goal of ennobling the mind. Each has its own methods, which aspire to transform our "negative imprints" into positive ones, so as to help us to make ourselves into happier beings. Buddhist teachings are complex, and it would be difficult to be a "part-time" Buddhist. Certainly it would be futile to try to become a Buddhist merely because it is in fashion.

To be Buddhist is also a state of mind. Some beings seem to have it naturally from birth, and know that they belong to this way, like a family of soul and spirit. It is like a relationship of love. One feels it in another, regardless of preconceived notions, even when that person is very different from what we would prefer or expect.

Buddhism is not based on magic or miracles. Although it makes radical demands, such as requiring us to "kill the very idea of the Buddha"—that is, to go beyond all our most cherished concepts, even that of the Buddha—we must first begin by taking the way suggested by Gautama Siddhartha Shakyamuni over 2,500 years ago.

No one else can do it for us.

HAPPINESS AND LOVE

Happiness

———

Our entire life is devoted to the search for happiness. Paradoxically, we constantly indulge in suffering.

In our Judaeo-Christian societies the idea of supreme happiness is often associated with a state of being which transpires essentially after death. It is only then, when our actions have been accounted and judged, that we can live forever in the paradise which the men of the Church have been telling us about for almost 2,000 years, and for which they are the intercessors. This particular map which links us to the cosmos is not one of stars and galaxies, but of sins, mortal or venial—sometimes alleviated by confession, but always surrounded by guilt.

Thus in our collective unconscious, earthly happiness is tinged with a quality of forbiddenness which arises from primordial, unchanging laws. Our human fears and terrors are welded into an iron collar which can actually be quite reassuring. The problem is that it also makes us forget our real mission, which is to grow up and be free. Free to really do good, and help others. Free to evolve in our own way, and thus capable of seeing through any system which cramps and hinders us, even when it has been accepted ever since earliest childhood, when we had neither the opportunity nor the right to test it for ourselves.

This morbid complicity with suffering runs deep in our culture. For example, until quite recently France was one of the European countries most reluctant to allow a medical patient to have morphine, even when they were experiencing excruciating pain. This cruelty has its origins in the notion that suffering is necessary in order to be delivered of this earthly burden of impulses and desires—a notion which has less and less credibility now.

The changes which began in May, 1968, plus scientific and medical progress, the opening of world borders through increased travel and migration, and the planetary intermingling of different cultures, have all been eroding these puritanical foundations for decades. As consumerism shows itself to be an illusory happiness, we seek other ways and means. We seek something which combines both earthly and spiritual happiness—assuming we believe in the reality of spirit. This happiness is our birthright, and we now demand it, along with its indispensable corollary of respect and love for others and for oneself.

In Buddhism the key to happiness is inseparably linked to what suffering has to teach us. This is not a teaching of punishment which brings redemption. It is a suffering which is understood, accepted, and recognized through all its disguises, so as not to fall back into being imprisoned in one's own habitual thoughts, actions, and words. It is this trap which is said to engender the unconscious cycle of rebirths.

The Buddha is often compared to a therapist. A healer of

body and soul, the Shakyamuni Buddha described a fourfold process of realization known as the Four Noble Truths. First, the diagnosis: great pain is an inescapable part of existence, for we must all endure (and see our loved ones endure) aging, infirmity, illness, and death. As long as we avoid this diagnosis, however subtly, we cannot be free of our pathology. But when we fully accept it, we enter the way which the Buddha calls the end of suffering, and can make genuine use of the skillful means that are then offered. Only after this acceptance can we become responsible for our seeking, instead of victims of it. Abandoning it leads to unconscious rebirth. Success is manifested in our way of being and perceiving the world, in our equanimity and peace of mind. Even in the midst of great trials, this quality of happiness is a radiance which belongs not only to ourselves, but to all beings.

Building Our Happiness

The key to our happiness is our ability to be content.

❧

Joy is power. Cultivate it!

❧

Life is like a dream, and one day you will have to awaken from it. Whether you experience a tremendous amount of happiness in this life, or only a little of it, it will appear just the same when you awaken: a hazy, fleeting memory, like that experienced in any dream. Whether our life is a long one or a short one, at the moment of death it is impossible to retain and preserve the same happiness we have experienced in our dream.

*

Our happiness is built from our everyday behavior and way of being, which induces either a feeling of contentment, or of frustration. The mind is the source of our attitude. And this mind is conditioned by its motivation—the key to all our behavior.

*

The longing of any lifetime is to realize happiness and to live in the joy and fullness which accompany it. It is possible to attain this, if we never give up hope in our ability to do so. Hope enables us to develop courage and to stop seeing existence as meaningless and devoid of purpose. This is vitally necessary for our own fulfillment, even with regard to very simple goals.

*

Without inner peace it is impossible to approach a difficult situation in a calm, detached, and balanced way. Inner peace protects your happiness and serenity. No matter what your material situation, if you do not have this peace, then you will be disturbed, worried, and unhappy when you encounter painful situations. Inner peace is the axis which determines your behavior.

❧

Authentic, lasting happiness depends upon causes and conditions which we have created. Unselfish acts are like seeds which fertilize our mind. The effects of these imprints facilitate the arrival of happy events.

❧

It is possible to live in a state of stable happiness only when we are completely free of ignorance. Awakening puts an end to unconscious rebirth, and then the conditions and causes of painful effects disappear. This is the realization of a state of happiness which no longer depends on our external circumstances, nor on our emotions.

❧

People often suppose that the realization of nirvana means the annihilation of all forms of existence. This is not true. What really transpires is that the illusions arising from our ignorance are extinguished, and we know true happiness, independent of any cause or condition. And we continue to exist.

❧

Worldly happiness is subject to our changing desires, and this is why it is unstable. The fundamental nature of desire is never to be satisfied. It always urges us to get and possess more and more. This perpetual discontent creates suffering, for the happiness that comes from consummation of pleasure is never lasting. We are afraid of seeing it go away, because we know how ephemeral it really is, and childishly suppose that if we can accumulate a large enough store of happy moments, then we will escape this effect. Thus the great diversity of objects upon which we project our fantasies and hopes turns out to be an endless source of frustration.

✺

True happiness does not depend on any external being or thing. It only depends on us.

✺

It is our actions, our words, and our thoughts which give rise to happiness or suffering. They are governed by our mind. If we transform our mind, we can realize happiness.

✺

It is we alone who have the power to build our happiness. But we must first examine the causes which will help us to develop and cultivate it. We must also proceed in the same manner in dealing with suffering. Once we know which things we need to either abandon or to encourage, we set in motion a process which leads to true happiness, and joy wells up spontaneously.

✺

Perfect peace can only be attained by pulling out our illusions by their roots.

✺

Sometimes it is necessary to sacrifice a small thing in order to obtain a greater one. If circumstances are favorable, and we are led to choose between our own happiness and the greater happiness of other beings, then we should not hesitate to choose the latter.

❧

The realization of authentic happiness requires a profound change in our way of thinking and in the way we see the world and others.

❧

We should never confuse happiness with pleasure.

❧

Knowing how to be content with what one has is a great joy in itself. This can only facilitate our further happiness.

❧

Our emotions are rooted in our sensations. Music influences our emotions. Certain forms of music connect us to subtle and profound realms of being. This can be a great help in learning happiness.

❧

Physical pleasure is short-lived. Happiness arises from the heart and the spirit.

❧

Happiness can be learned. And it should be, for it is a necessary apprenticeship. It shows us how decisive positive emotions are in our life and its fulfillment.

❧

If we wish to avoid the occurrence of a disagreeable event in our daily life, we must be serious about recognizing and renouncing the chain of habitual causes and conditions which bring it about. Conversely, if we wish to attract the occurrence of a happy event, we must set in motion a process of causes and conditions which favor it. We are all subject to this law of causality.

❧

Attaining happiness means facilitating the causes and conditions which produce it. Renouncing suffering means eliminating, as much as possible, the causes and conditions which produce it.

❧

To choose happiness as the goal of our existence is to undergo a major transformation in the way we live.

❧

In fact, happiness *is* the real goal of our life. We all want to be happy. The authentic movement of our life naturally pulls us toward happiness. Let us do everything in our power to pay attention to this movement in every moment, so as to arrive there.

❧

By skillful exercise of the mind, we can realize happiness.

❧

Skillful exercise of the mind is a discipline which includes intellect, feeling, heart, and spirit. This inner discipline helps us to change our attitude, our concepts, and our entire way of seeing our existence. In the beginning, it teaches us to discriminate among the factors which lead either to happiness or to suffering. After this, there only remains the work of cultivating those which are sources of happiness.

❧

Athletic activity affects both body and mind. Creativity and intelligence can flourish with its help. Sports are among the skillful means which facilitate the discovery of happiness.

❧

Four factors are necessary for the realization of individual happiness: inner richness; the meeting of basic material needs; a spiritual path; and the experience of awakening.

❧

If we subscribe to a strictly materialist worldview, then a number of preconditions are necessary before we can even begin to cultivate joy and happiness in everyday life: good health, financial security, material comfort, friends, an intimate partner....

❧

The key, the very essence, of a happy life is our state of mind.

❧

It is a mistake to think that happiness and peace of mind make one indifferent to others and to the world. Such an absolute detachment would not be true peace of mind, for the latter is nourished by love and compassion.

*

If you have inner peace and equanimity, then nothing can disturb you deeply. You can experience full happiness no matter what the circumstances. But if you lack inner peace and equanimity, then even the most fortunate and comfortable circumstances will give you no lasting happiness. The stability which is inherent in inner peace is the true source of happiness.

*

The goal of our existence is to find happiness and to live fully and with satisfaction. Yet great trials, sorrows, and pains are inescapable. It is imperative to face these in a concrete and realistic way, if we are not to be overwhelmed by the problems associated with them.

Happiness Is to Be Shared

Every human being has a right to be happy, including criminals in prison. Prisons are necessary, but we must change our views of those who are paying their debt to society in this way. We need to be more tolerant, and to stop excluding and rejecting them.

❧

All sentient beings, including even the smallest animals, have some sense of an independent "me." The true nature of this "self" is very rarely realized. Nevertheless, all these vast multitudes of big and small selves have one thing in common: the desire to be happy and to avoid suffering. The entire universe is driven by this quest.

❧

If we have learned to discipline our own minds, to be content with what we possess, and to live in peace with others and with ourselves, we will be happy even if our conditions of life worsen. Furthermore, others around us will aid and support us, because we have been kind and generous with them.

❧

Rejoice in others' happiness!

❦

The truly virtuous are those who give happiness both to others and to themselves. Every moment matters, and it is of little importance whether the happiness is intermittent or constant.

❦

If a person expresses something positive, support it. If they perform a good act, congratulate them. Do not hesitate to praise them to others in their absence. Take pleasure in hearing others appreciated. If someone says something good about someone you know, do not hesitate to join them in it.

❦

If someone congratulates you, praises you, or extols your attitude, your first reaction should be to ascertain whether these words of praise are accurate or not. If they are, then avoid all pride, and simply appreciate that your merits have been recognized.

❦

It is lamentable to regard an animal primarily as a source of food. Animals are also sentient beings whom we should care for. Just like us, they hold onto dear life and want to preserve their "self." The pain they experience when they are hunted, fished, or led to the slaughterhouse is undeniable. When we reflect deeply on their suffering, we become appalled at the idea of eating them. If our conditions of life and environment allow us to stay healthy by feeding ourselves in a different way, then it is better to be vegetarian. We should never ignore the current immeasurable suffering of animals on this planet.

Love without attachment, free of the craving which binds us, springs from a wholehearted wish for all beings to realize happiness. This quality of love fosters an equanimity of being, receiving, and giving which recognizes all being as one. It is a giving of oneself to all, especially to other sentient beings, whether humans, animals, spirits, gods, angels, or to those hungry ghosts which inhabit the hell-realms.

This wish, born of a radiant and generous spirit, is the foundation of the Bodhisattva Way. But it is not enough to wish it. This opening toward others must not become just an intellectual philosophy, for then it would never get beyond mere speculation and well-wishing. It must manifest as action in order to live. Its energy and authenticity are sustained by our daily acts, thoughts, and feelings.

Our inner conditions produce our outer world, and what we make of it. This is where our real power lies: in transforming ourselves so as to be able to participate in the lives of all beings everywhere, from those close to us to those we dislike, and not excluding beings who are very far away and different in scale, even the tiniest cell. All beings are linked, interdependent, and in constant relationship. To help them to be free of the causes of suffering is the path of Love. Deep commitment is needed in order to take this path, for one must follow it without any expectation of reward.

In order to go beyond our limitations, our selfishness, fear, and attachments, it is very helpful to remember the teaching that others are also ourselves. Thus every spark of love that flies from us to others is also—and immediately—a gift and blessing for us as well. If we remind ourselves of this by constantly bearing in mind the mantra: "I am others, and others are myself," so that it is finally seen as self-evident, the light and force that fill us will overflow in scintillating streams of love.

Love

My only religion is love.

✿

My practice of love is built on compassion, joy, and impartiality.

✿

There are two types of love:
—That which is subjective, and dependent upon emotion, affection, and attachment which we experience with lovers, friends, family, and others close to us.
—That which arises from awareness and contemplation of the truth that all beings desire happiness. We are all equals with regard to this longing. The feeling of affinity which this engenders leads us toward a profound desire and will for all beings to be happy. Then we experience true love.

❧

Maternal love and compassion are deeply woven into the bonds between parents and their newborn child. This type of love is essentially independent of emotional attachment. A mother loves and is responsible for her infant, and simply does everything she can to assure its well-being. It is a form of love which is devoid of self-interest and expectation. Authentic compassion is similar to maternal love in this sense, for it is a love which goes beyond personal preference, and even beyond friendship and enmity. When dealing with enemies, if you are attentive to their suffering and longing, even though they are trying to harm you; if you try to help them despite their bad actions, yet without allowing them to overcome you; then you will realize authentic love and compassion.

❧

From conception to birth, a mother should live as peacefully and calmly as possible. Her happiness will help the baby to develop harmoniously. After birth, nursing is the most important act. Milk is the physical symbol of true love, which enables us to survive and grow. The physical affection between mother and child has been the subject of medical studies, which show that frequent affectionate contact with the mother, or her substitute, is vital for the development of the child's brain and nervous system.

❧

Some couple relationships are overly dependent upon a strong and immediate sexual attraction. Such a desire-dominated bond nurtures extreme emotionality. Like anger, hatred, or thirst for revenge, such impulses can lead one to succumb to madness. Ravaged by extreme polarities, such couples are easily broken.

This type of relationship demands prompt satisfaction of one's physical desire by the other. This imperative becomes basic to the functioning of the couple, and leads to regarding the other as an object of desire and satisfaction. This can never be the basis of an authentic rapport with another. This is why such couples are so unstable, and often divorce. If you build your house upon a bank of snow, should you be surprised when the weather changes and it melts?

❧

An authentic couple relationship may involve a powerful sexual attraction, but the physical aspect is not the primary thing. Mutual respect is more important, for then the other person is not regarded as an object. This kind of relationship needs time, so as to get to know and understand each other, and to learn how to love authentically.

❧

A durable couple relationship is built upon a sense of responsibility, and the desire for long-term commitment. Although the sexual aspect offers immediate pleasure and satisfaction, it is also a biological function which has long-term consequences when children are conceived. It is of fundamental importance to accept full responsibility and commitment toward children before having them.

❧

The constant search for romantic love can be a serious obstacle in one's spiritual development and flowering. This idealization of love is in some way connected with an extreme need which clouds one's perception of reality, one's attention in the present, and the nature of one's affection for the other. Like all fantasy, it is by nature difficult or impossible to realize. This can lead to extreme frustration, and a great waste of time and energy.

❧

Love which grows between two beings who respect each other is a form of knowledge.

True compassion can arise from the feeling of closeness which this engenders. This affection is authentic and spontaneous, for it is free of all expectation and self-interest.

❧

Equanimity is like a good, smooth soil which has been fertilized by loving kindness. The experience of equanimity implies the ability to feel an impartial, genuine love for all beings and to act accordingly.

❧

There are two approaches in the learning of universal Love:
—One which consists in recognizing and accepting that, in the infinite scale of all our transmigrational cycles, every being we encounter has, at one time or another, been our parent. Knowing this, we can only be moved by their suffering or torment,

———

and desire to help them.

—Another approach is based on reflection. This involves a lucid appraisal of the disadvantages of selfishness compared with the advantages of generosity and selflessness. This reasoning leads us to see that others are as important as ourselves, and that it is appropriate to love them as we would like to be loved.

Whichever of these two approaches is right for us will be determined by our own beliefs, and our ability to change our state of mind.

❧

True love can neither alter nor disappear, since it arises from selflessness rather than from attachment and desire.

2

EMOTIONS

Our Western tendency to systematize everything often leads to confusion when we think about emotions. When it is pointed out to us that we are manipulated and destabilized by our own emotions, and that it is possible to undertake a work to free ourselves from their yoke, we tend to conclude that this work must involve suppressing them.

Buddhism is known as the Middle Way, more subtle and effective than any extremist way. Thus it is recognized that emotions remain necessary, even for living Buddhas. Compassion is the foundation of the noblest emotions, an indispensable element of the life of the spirit, both seed and ground of the realization of our true nature, which is also that of all beings.

Tara, a feminine divinity, symbolizes for Tibetan Buddhists the power and indestructible force of compassion. Both protective mother and energy in action, to invoke her in the midst of difficulties is enough to propel the believer right to the heart of her mandala, the cosmos in which she surrounds and aids each individual. She is the universal Mother, a powerful archetype recognized in all religious traditions. In Christianity, Mary occupies this same space and plays this same role as "Mother of God."

Tara is known as consoler as well as protector, and alleviates the sufferings of humanity. This exoteric aspect should not blind us to a more subtle and inner interpretation. Tara is also an aspect of our own Spirit, embodying one of its many possible manifestations.

Like other mythic figures, divinities arise and have their meaning in realms beyond the limits of conceptual thought. Beyond literal words which define, enclose, and distort these realms, visual and auditory activities which evoke specific divinities operate directly upon more subtle levels of our being.

At least in theory, there is no sexual inequality in Buddhism. As Goddess, Tara is just as important as any masculine representation. She also has an origin-story, for Tibetans like to associate their mythic symbols with such a story. Although belonging to the mythic and imaginal realm, she becomes more accessible to our reality by having a source, with an origin-story. This origin is none other than Avalokiteshvara, the Buddha of Compassion. Having made an extreme effort to save all beings from suffering, he thought he had won. But when he opened his eyes once more upon this universe he had just saved, he saw that suffering was beginning to fill it again. A tear of sadness and another tear of discouragement ran down his cheeks. Two great queens were touched by these tears, and were transformed into the dual manifestations of the Goddess Tara: the Green Tara and the White Tara, who are in reality one. Tara is also considered as the mother of all Buddhas.

Compassion, Giving, Selflessness, and Kindness

———

Compassion dissolves and banishes fear.

When we allow true compassion and kindness to grow in us, we offer them the space that was formerly occupied by fear. When fear gives way, confidence and inner peace can flourish.

❧

True compassion is already an element of our fundamental nature. But this potential we all possess is not actualized until we develop it and live it.

Compassion and hatred are opposite and incompatible feelings. They can never simultaneously occupy the space of our mind. If one is active, the other is inactive. Thus when we are possessed by hatred, it is impossible to feel compassion. And a feeling which is not active and present in us remains merely a virtual sentiment, an unused potential.

❧

Within the most cruel and perverse human being, there is a grain of love and compassion. It is this grain which will make them into a Buddha some day.

❧

Selflessness has two aspects: loving others; and acting with compassion and kindness.

The first aspect requires loving oneself. Self-love—if it is genuine, and not egoistic—enables us to find the confidence and courage which will help us to develop and establish relationships of love with others.

The second aspect is helping others. But here again, we must not forget that we are also beings in need of help. If we are to help others, it is vital to learn how to help ourselves.

❧

When I speak of the Buddhas and the great spiritual masters, I sometimes say that they represent the perfection of selfishness. Indeed, it is because of their boundless love and selflessness with regard to others that they were able realize their own awakening, their own freedom from suffering, and their own knowledge of perfect happiness.

This supreme expression of "selfishness" is dynamic and serviceable—and of course very different from the forms of selfishness that we ordinarily see. The latter limit and confine us, making us stupid, stubborn, and narrow-minded.
Thus the lives of the great masters demonstrate that if we wish to be happy, it is necessary to develop true compassion.
However, we should seriously question any "compassion" which makes us more unhappy.

❧

Cultivating compassion does not mean adding your own suffering to that of others.

❧

True compassion does not mean suffering in the place of the other person. If we try to help someone, and their suffering invades us, we are being ineffective. To persist in this only reinforces the ego.

❧

Only human beings are able to cultivate selflessness and kindness. This ability should be practiced every day.

❧

Why take the trouble to increase our compassion? Because we are aware and concerned by others' suffering—and we have discovered that this provides us with the means to help them.

❧

True compassion can never be forced upon us, because it requires the agreement of our reflection and will. In contrast to this, "ordinary" suffering overwhelms the mind when a painful situation occurs, often causing despair because it arrives so abruptly and unexpectedly.

❧

It is through reflection that we develop our will and determination to follow certain practices. For example, let us examine the basis of the benefits which come from giving. When we give, we respond to the needs of those who have less than us. Thus we contribute, according to our capacity, to the alleviation of their suffering. Their well-being also gives us an immense feeling of satisfaction and joy. And since this joy gives rise to peace and serenity, it helps both us and others to be more happy. Our happiness is deeply connected with that of others.

❧

Compassion is non-violent by nature. Its fundamental motivation is the wish to see all beings free of suffering. This wish becomes effective when our commitment leads to an evolved sense of responsibility and to feeling and demonstrating respect for others.

❧

Compassion which is the result of attachment is not authentic. As soon as the object of attachment "abandons" us, we revile and reject the bond we had imagined. Then the typical reaction is one of resentment, anger, and even hatred.

❧

If we observe that our feeling of compassion depends on our projections onto the person who is loved, we can be certain that this love is just an ordinary attachment—only a partial love.

❧

Authentic compassion is simple, strong, profound, and stable.
   Love which springs from this compassion has the same qualities.

❧

The more we understand and deeply know the nature of suffering and its varied manifestations, the greater our capacity to feel compassion.

❧

What helps us to act, instead of merely reacting, is the full and conscious knowledge of what compassion really is.

❧

If you experience great suffering, and indulge in the feeling of how unjust it is, then you allow it to dominate you. You will feel powerless, overwhelmed, and unable to react appropriately.

❧

When you are first learning to cultivate compassion, you may often experience a kind of uneasiness in the face of others' suffering. This is only a temporary phase. It is simply a sign that you do not yet know the full meaning of the experience of compassion.

❧

To voluntarily accept another's suffering, and make every effort to help them, develops spiritual strength and an unexpected force of determination.

❧

The desire to approach another and to communicate with them, to help them without patronizing them, awakens an immense energy and great joy in us, which banishes weariness.

❧

The true value of existence is revealed through compassion.

❧

It is compassion that assures humanity's survival.

❧

Those who are deprived of charity and compassion are constantly prey to fear, dissatisfaction, and gloom. They then become merciless, for these negative emotions afflict them constantly and excessively, even in their sleep.

Those who are capable of compassion experience a feeling of freedom and confidence which allows them to relax and be happy in all kinds of situations.

❧

We should use every moment to practice the abilities of our compassionate nature. Who can say what its limits are? It doesn't matter, for the important thing is to go as far as we can in mobilizing these abilities. Then we will have no regrets, knowing that we have done our best to help make this world a better place.

❧

To generate compassion in ourselves, it is enough to simply recognize the truth that happiness is our birthright.

❧

Imagine, visualize, and feel what someone who is suffering

feels. Analyze the reasons for their suffering. Try to establish a link with this person. Remember that their capacity for suffering is similar to yours; that their desire to be free of this negative emotion is the same as yours.

Then you can truly choose to help them, so that they no longer experience this distress. The love and compassion which flow from this decision manifest first in your own mind. Then you can live this and apply it in your daily life.

*

It is easier to communicate with others if we demonstrate compassion, affection, and kindness. This openness and availability are also the keys to our inner world.

*

The love and compassion we give to others help us to free ourselves of our own negative emotions.

*

Our physiological and emotional balance depends on our ability to give, to love, and to experience compassion.

*

We cannot satisfy the demands of immature and unreasonable people. To frequent their company is usually a waste of time. However, it is important to understand that they act as slaves of their emotions and passions. This is why we should still feel loving kindness for them.

*

A word of kindness is sweet, calm, clear, and agreeable to hear.

❧

Our capacity for selflessness grows without limits if we develop our resolve to practice virtue. This is how a virtual ability becomes a real ability.

❧

Nothing can unsettle authentic compassion; not even hostility or hatred aimed at us.

❧

The essential is to be kind, selfless, and generous throughout one's life.

❧

Without compassion, peace would collapse immediately around the world.

❧

Illusion, violence, and craving for power are at the root of most problems we encounter. Love and compassion are the remedies for these spiritual poisons. The moral thread which maintains world peace depends upon these remedies.

❧

Compassion is not an infantile characteristic.
    Nor is it sentimental.
    It is not based on our attachments and desires.
    To recognize its true nature is to activate it, and this can

lead to developing this potential which we all possess.

Our behavior toward others will then be transformed.

❧

By dissolving our fears, compassion opens us to the world.

❧

True compassion is spontaneous, whole, universal. It is ageless and measureless, neither subjective nor emotional.

❧

Authentic compassion expects nothing in return.

❧

Compassion has an infinite variety of manifestations. It is based on our sense of belonging to the universe, and it includes all beings.

❧

In the beginning, compassion is not yet steadfast and spontaneous. It must be generated and cultivated through long meditations.

❧

We humans are all similar, and equal in our deepest being. Today more than ever, the images we receive from all over the planet demonstrate this fundamental unity. This exposes the absurdity of racist notions, and compels us to develop universal compassion.

Fear, Anger, Hatred, Jealousy, Pride, and Violence

———

When we see our enemies showered with praise, fame, or happiness, it is as if we were pierced by arrows. And when we see them condemned or struck by misfortune, we feel gratified.

❧

Are we only gratified by personal praise directed to us? Then there is something not right. It shows our immaturity.

❧

It is all too easy to let ourselves to be invaded by aggression and violence. We should be mindful of the danger of being overtaken by these toxic emotions.

❧

Hatred and violence are worthless, either for individuals or for nations. We must do away with the notion that they can ever be advantageous before we can live in mutual respect and non-violence.

❧

Violence gives rise to violence.

❧

Reinforcement of the "ego," and of the image we have of our "self," makes us more and more aggressive and violent. This

———

process increases the conflict we experience with those around us.

❧

The death penalty is an extreme form of violence. It is useless, reckless, and ignorant. Like all violence, it generates other violence. It is preferable to imprison a person for life than to cancel their right to live.

❧

Every form of violence that can be avoided, should be.

❧

Killing animals is a form of violence which disturbs universal harmony. When we act in this way, we affect the balance of the cosmos.

❧

It is useless to wish we were less violent, hateful, and aggressive. Mere wishing does not disperse anger when it overcomes us. It overlooks the universal principle of cause and effect which is always operating in our lives, working through our body, our words, our thoughts, and our actions.

❧

When our mind is invaded by destructive emotions, it comes under their control. It is already too late to prevent their effects. We must act before these emotions take us over, by analyzing the causes which nurture them.

❧

The constant ambition to achieve more in our career or social status may increase our power, but to the detriment of others.

❧

The thirst for power increases our ability to compete against other human beings. It arises from our belief in our identity as separate beings, existing independently of them. This thirst is often aroused by envy. It can make us condescending, even arrogant towards anyone who crosses our path.

❧

Hatred plunges us into torment, ravaging our inner life. It engenders complex and burdensome emotions. And it creates ever more misery in our daily life.

❧

The motivation behind an act is essential. It is prior to the movement which manifests itself in outer acts. Only a virtuous motivation, based on goodwill toward others, can counteract negative emotions such as fear, anxiety, anger, or hostility.

❧

Others' opinions of you are of little importance when you practice being kind, generous, selfless, and compassionate. When you know you are giving your best effort in this regard, no setback can disturb your inner peace. And you will not be forever deliberating about the validity of your goals.

❧

If you remain under the spell of your negative emotions, it will be impossible to realize your aims. These emotions are a kind of involuntary, self-inflicted torture. They can destroy you.

❧

Some people work hard to earn money. Others become aggressive and dishonest in search of it. All of them become more and more hypnotized by mediocre, banal activities. Ultimately, they may allow all their time to be devoured by these, and yet feel no revulsion.

❧

If you lack self-confidence, and feel self-loathing rather than self-love, then stop thinking about the painful aspects of your life. Think instead of this fantastic human potential that dwells within you. It only asks to be developed.

❧

Just as fire needs fuel in order to burn, so aversion needs an object in order to manifest.

❧

The underlying causes of annoyance and irritability are several. Among them are fear and anxiety. These cause us to react unconsciously to certain events in our lives.

❧

It is easier to get angry at someone than to try to understand the reasons why we become irritated and upset.

§

People who have lost their house in a fire become very vigilant about the danger of fire and its causes. You should be just as aware of the destruction wrought by the fires of hatred.

If you meet someone who incites real hatred in you, remove yourself from the danger. Do not allow yourself to catch on fire.

§

Someone expresses unpleasant and insulting opinions about you, and you feel attacked and injured. This slander destroys your peace of mind. And you react. If you can, ignore such insults. In this way, you will avoid setting in motion the causes of new suffering.

§

Social conditioning encourages you to retaliate when someone slanders you or wrongs you in some way. But if you truly want to transform your mind, it is always better to let go of the thirst for victory—leave that to the other.

§

Often when we give comfort or aid to someone, we expect and hope that someday they will give us something in return when the occasion arises. If they fail to do this, we feel it is unfair. Our tendency is then to react, to criticize, to demand. However, try a different way of thinking about it: that this individual may in fact be a teacher for you. He or she is show-ing you how to give without attachment. And then concen-trate on the good things about this person.

❧

If jealousy, pride, aversion, hostility, and resentment grow in us, our happiness is destroyed. Others then appear hostile and aggressive to us. And this sets up inhibitions, fears, and self-centeredness.

❧

Tolerance is also a discipline. It implies a willing choice to turn away from all the many possible acts of revenge, harm, and violence.

❧

Depression and despondency are extreme emotional expres-sions. Hatred is even more extreme. This is why it is so terri-ble and dangerous in its consequences.

❧

A Buddhist teaching says that harboring hatred is like thrust-ing a sword into the front of your belly in order to stab some-one standing behind you.

❧

Outer disarmament will not be achieved until there is inner disarmament.

❧

To know and accept one's limits is essential. This enables us to set attainable goals, avoiding failures and frustration.

❧

Nothing justifies pride. It is based on an overestimation of oneself. Pride and self-confidence are totally different things. Self-confidence is founded on real self-knowledge. This is why it assures us of success.

❧

Our faculty of judgment is destroyed by hatred and violence. In such moments of madness, anything can happen. Only a calm and balanced mind is able to deal with all situations.

❧

It is common to criticize, accuse, and disparage ourselves. These are forms of anger directed inward. We blame our faults, our inadequacies, our limitations. We talk to our "self" as if we were two separate entities. But we know this is not true. The only thing about this pretense that can be constructive and healthy is to use it so as to continually re-question ourselves as to who we really are.

❧

We must develop our self-clarity and skills of critical analysis by contemplating our multiplicity: we are composed of many aspects.

❧

If anger, hostility, and other negative emotions were really built-in expressions of the human mind, it would be useless to attempt to transform them. But long experience has proven that it is entirely possible to do away with them, vanquishing ignorance and gaining knowledge.

✣

If pride grows in us when we experience success and good fortune, it is urgent to remind ourselves of the more painful aspects of our existence, and to be mindful of suffering. This keeps our feet on the ground.

✣

Most Tibetans do not experience self-hatred. This is surely because they engage in a daily contemplation—especially during the practice of meditation—of their real potential as human beings. With this awareness of who they really are on the deepest level, it is difficult for them to give any credence to notions of their own worthlessness. This is why they make such great efforts to live in accord with this practice.

Attachment and Craving

All our errors have their roots in craving and aversion. These are our fundamental illusions. The only way to counteract them is to apply a specific antidote. For example, you can develop patience with your enemies, with those who wrong you, or with those who bore and annoy you. When the anti-dote of patience is working, aversion cannot arise.

❧

Attachment, craving, and aversion give rise to great emotional troubles. These disturbances eclipse our ability to find solutions to problems that arise.

❧

Craving is insatiable, and its possible objects are endless. To devote yourself to consummating it is to condemn yourself to always be wanting more, for nothing can really satisfy it. It is like drinking salty water when you are thirsty: it only leaves you more thirsty, and impairs your well-being.

❧

Sensual pleasures are like honey covering the blade of a sword. Seeking them can engender perpetual dissatisfaction.

❧

When desires such as those for peace, for happiness, or for a better world find a good channel of expression, they are beneficial desires. However, beware of allowing them to become obsessive: this leads to many troubles.

❧

Our perpetual dissatisfaction inculcates the desire to experience situations which are extreme and overpowering.

❧

All extremist and fanatic thoughts come from cramped attitudes.

❧

What makes a desire positive is not the pleasure of its fulfillment, but its far-reaching consequences. When certain desires—for example, to have more and more possessions—run up against the limits imposed by reality, we become depressed. This is because of our inability to be satisfied with what we have.

❧

Greed is always connected with inflated expectation. It always creates frustration, because it is impossible to satisfy in the long run. When we become conscious of this, we can employ its antidote: contentment. This enables us to be happy with what we already possess.

❧

The medicine which helps us to go beyond our worldly desires is insight into the illusory, impermanent nature of all phenomena, which are certain to change. When we understand that all things are interdependent, we see into their true nature. This can help us to free ourselves from the desire to acquire and possess, which manipulates us through our ego.

❧

It is partly our social context which defines our desires as positive or negative. Take the automobile for example: in a prosperous consumer society, wanting to have a car is considered to be a positive thing. But in a poor village in India, where a car is unnecessary for most people, such a purchase could easily cause envy and lead to many unpleasant complications.

❧

People are fascinated by money, gambling, drugs, and many other desires rooted in sensation. These things offer occasional pleasure. But how can such fleeting satisfaction be a worthwhile goal in itself?

❧

Work on the mind especially requires that we not open the door to craving and greed, for these are our most ferocious enemies.

❧

Our power over things and other people is as intoxicating as any drug. This is why we so often give in to this desire. It clouds our awareness of inner peace. We then project our thirst for power onto more and more objects of conquest. We no longer take the time to wonder whether we find any genuine happiness in the pleasures which result. Yet such questioning is a real necessity, for it renews our consciousness of this fundamental truth: as long as there is concord between a desire and its object, we can and often do experience satisfaction from practically anything.

❧

Satisfaction of sexual craving implies the feeling of possessing the other. This is only a mental projection, because it distorts the reality of the relationship.

❧

When our desire for a loved one fades, our whole view of that person may be transformed. Sometimes this change happens so suddenly that it astonishes us. In such a case, the desire had been eclipsing the true nature of the other and of the relationship. Such desire is maintained by mutual ignorance of the other's true nature.

Patience, Humility, and Tolerance

Tolerance for those who have done us wrong does not mean submitting to injustice. It does mean cultivating a different way of acting, one which is free of all negative emotions such as hostility or hatred.

❧

Patience is the indispensable means for overcoming suffering.

❧

To be patient implies freedom from aggression and anger. It means not harboring seeds of hatred, even toward those who have hurt us and want to destroy us. However, patience does not mean acceptance of an adversary's abusive behavior. Consider the situation of Tibetans, for example. If we respond with violence to the oppression and torture, this reaction will ultimately harm us more. On the other hand, if we have developed patience in ourselves, we can struggle more effectively against injustice and bear more powerful witness to the violence committed against us.

❧

The noblest form of patience is to accept trials with joy. It is this kind of patience which helps us to attain real perseverance. In this way we realize our true nature as human beings.

❧

Any person who causes us to develop our capacity for patience should be regarded as a friend.

❧

If we really succeed in loving our enemies as friends and teachers, we will be finished with all relationship problems. Then we can develop our sense of universal responsibility toward all living beings.

❧

Patience enables us to remove all blocks to development of our compassion.

❧

Patience is power. It springs from our deep capacity to remain strong and unshaken, no matter what the circumstances.

❧

We are truly humble when we are able to not react to a situation which tempts us with an opportunity to solve things in a violent manner.

❧

If we feel so powerless and deprived that we have no choice but to submit to whatever happens to us without reacting, then we certainly do not possess true humility.

❧

Empty chatter is based only on desire, aversion, agreement, and disagreement. It is a useless activity.

❧

If someone does something which seems unjust or unacceptable to you, remember that their action is part of a chain of cause and effect which is independent of their will. They are not free of their emotions, so why get upset over their actions? If they were not enslaved by their emotions, then they would have chosen to cause only happiness, for our common desire is to avoid unhappiness.

❧

If you retaliate with violence when an enemy mistreats you, you are both wrong. Do not react like this. Never forget that the suffering you experience is conditioned by your past actions. Given this, then why be upset by someone who is only the vehicle for revealing this? The negative imprints you create have effects, and these will continue to manifest until they completely exhaust themselves.

❧

What good does it really do you to feel glad when your enemy suffers? What can wishing for your enemy's unhappiness give you? This wish will have no effect on their life, even if it appears that their pain and distress resulted from it.

❧

When you enter a spiritual path, your enemies become a decisive factor in your practice. Each of them represents a unique opportunity and an aid to your progress in developing patience, tolerance, love, and compassion. Your friends cannot help you as effectively to cultivate that spiritual resolve and power known as patience. Only your enemies have the ability to educate you in this.

❧

In developing an attitude of impartiality and equality toward all beings, our goal is not to become indifferent or insensitive. The primary thing is to lay a new foundation, creating a space of freedom in our mind. It is from this space that we will be able to generate positive thoughts and emotions.

❧

It may happen that in spite of all your efforts, you are unable to see the good qualities of another person—in such a case, it is better to refrain from thinking about them at all, so as to avoid harboring negative emotions.

❧

It is normal to feel resentment toward someone who has hurt you and made you suffer. It is also quite human to feel sympathy and affection for someone who makes you happy by giving you what you want. But if we desire to develop equanimity, and transform this partiality into impartiality, we must make use of special and precise techniques.

❧

An enemy is like a rare and precious asset. We should rejoice at the prospect of such a treasure appearing among the people we know. For if we succeed in our practice of developing patience and tolerance, thanks are due as much to our enemies as to our own efforts.

❧

Love and tenderness go along with tolerance. Real tolerance is strength, and has nothing to do with weakness or lack of courage and determination. Being tolerant does not mean giving in to injustice. On the contrary, it means finding solutions which enable us to stop submitting to suffering. It does this by helping us to end all forms of bias, ill-will, and indulgence of emotions such as anger and hatred. It is the absence of these negative emotions that sharply distinguishes authentic tolerance from mere politeness resulting from social training. We can only be said to have developed authentic tolerance when we are capable of love, compassion, selflessness, and good actions, instead of violence, when we are faced with injustice. We are truly tolerant when we can remain emotionally calm, yet neither indifferent nor insensitive.

Suffering

———

We often lie in order to deny suffering. This is unacceptable. On the other hand, if we have to lie in order to save a life, or to protect people or spiritual teachings, the consequences are totally different. Everything depends on the motivation which is behind the lie.

❦

Be mindful of your smallest faults, for they are karmic tendencies. These past imprints feed habits which must be abandoned.

❦

All phenomena are illusory. However, do not neglect to decode the messages which they address to you through your experience.

It is futile to deny the existence of suffering when it manifests itself in our life. Although this manifestation induces us to believe in the reality of suffering, the whole thing is really dreamlike in nature. Just as in a dream, the identity we assume is an illusion, yet the distress feels quite real to us. Understanding the deceptive character of phenomena makes it easier for us to confront the difficulties we experience.

❦

Situations that cause suffering outnumber those that cause happiness.

———

Whether we like it or not, suffering is an integral part of our existence. The only way to bear it is to transform our attitude with regard to it. Struggling constantly against suffering only increases and reinforces it. The same principle applies to an insomniac who becomes tense in an effort to sleep. If we worry and cannot accept the fact that sleep is evading us, our stress increases and the night is interminably long.

❧

No one likes to suffer. But to stop rebelling against this state enables us to transform our mind and our behavior. Then it is easier to deal with suffering.

❧

There are two ways of reacting psychologically to a painful situation:
— Becoming anxious and agitated. This state of mind favors the growth of worry, fear, doubt, and frustration. It may finally lead to depression, and even suicidal tendencies.
— Reacting constructively by examining the causes and conditions which have permitted such a situation to arise. We then learn a lesson from this experience, becoming more pragmatic and in tune with reality.

❧

Our immaturity is the cause of our unhappiness. This childishness conditions us, so that we mull over unimportant events and focus our attention on details which induce great suffering. It is essential to change our outlook so as to dwell only upon that which gives real meaning to our existence.

❧

Wisdom consists in regarding every difficult and painful circumstance as a vehicle of evolution on our spiritual path. Pain has other aspects besides the negative ones. If we wish great inner transformation to take place in us, it is indispensable.

❧

Learning self-mastery is a process which applies to all domains. For example, learning about the nature of suffering begins with bearing small pains. Then it becomes easier to deal with much greater ones.

❧

The soul-strength and self-mastery we gain from bearing up under hardships empowers us to face any situation without letting ourselves be crushed.

❧

Every trial which occurs on a spiritual path has a meaning. We must seek it and find it.

❧

In order to eliminate laziness, we must first know its causes. Among these is the pleasure we take in wasting our time — in daydreaming, unconsciousness, escapism, and in our indifference toward others' suffering.

❧

It is striking and paradoxical that, even though our body wears out with age, disturbing and negative emotions can be felt with the same intensity as before. The power of these emotions is not diminished by the mere passage of time.

❧

Thinking about our suffering and the relative nature of existence puts an end to pride and arrogance. This reflection opens us to others. We consider their needs, their pain, and their anguish. Our compassionate nature awakens, and we become aware of how urgent it is to diminish and abandon our negative actions, so as to stop experiencing their consequences. We then give priority to positive attitudes which engender joy and happiness.

❧

Ignorance—in other words, lack of knowledge of our fundamental nature—is the root of suffering.

❧

There are two stages in the analysis of suffering which are necessary and indispensable if we want to rid our lives of it, and renounce all craving:
—First, identify the suffering in question.
—Second, understand its origin and the causes and conditions which have allowed it to manifest.

❧

Pain is inseparable from existence. Only when we accept this fact are we able to understand its true nature. Then it is possible to recognize the mechanisms at work, and be prepared for them.

❧

To look deeply into the real nature of our suffering would be harmful, a mere exercise in masochism and morbidity, if we did not have the power to transform it.

❧

You are in danger when you allow sorrow, sadness, anxiety, fear, and discouragement to invade you, isolating you and amplifying your self-centeredness. If you harbor an image of yourself as victim, you will become self-absorbed and depressive. When such trials come, think of others who have been through similar, and worse, hardships. This will be of great help to you.

❧

Suffering will continue to permeate all our existences as long as we have not realized true awakening. Pain and grief are built into this world of cycles. When we feel emotional or physical pain, a reaction of aversion immediately sets in. Suffering is essentially connected to this rejection of pain. They are causally related, because the pain appears unfair, not right. It is possible to greatly reduce the intensity of your distress if you see how you are indulging and depending on this suffering, and agree to abandon it.

❧

Contemplation of the nature and causes of suffering enables you to see that you have the choice to be free of it.

❦

We often unconsciously feed and intensify negative emotions, creating suffering and provoking emotional disturbances and certain physical disorders. But if we embrace an attitude which places the painful experience in a more relative perspective, it will help diminish the duration and intensity of these moments. In this way we avoid stirring up new negative emotions whose only function is to reinforce the others.

❦

Psychological suffering and happiness are more profound and intense than physical suffering and happiness.

❦

Our experiences of pain, suffering, pleasure, and happiness are partly mind-generated. But we must not jump to the conclusion that reality is based only on the activity of our mind.

❦

If solutions do indeed exist for transforming and mastering painful situations, then we must dedicate ourselves to discovering and applying them. Yet there will always be sorrows which are unavoidable and impossible to control. With these, we must transform our mind so as to view them in a concrete and realistic way. Then it is possible to bear them as they occur. This attitude is both an aid and a protection for us. Of course we can't expect it to make a physical pain disappear—but it will enable us to rid the experience of physical pain of the useless psychological suffering which is added onto it.

❧

"Birth, aging, separation from loved ones, illness, and unrealized desires." According to the teaching of the Buddha, these are the inescapable realities of this world, upon which our suffering is built. It manifests itself in all sorts of ways, physical, mental, and emotional.

❧

Craving creates suffering.

Craving rages like fire, inflaming the senses toward one object of desire after another. Illusion then reigns supreme, devouring us like a permanent conflagration.

It is this blaze that we must extinguish.

3

THE OTHER

Attraction and repulsion, love and hate, desire and indifference, lust and rejection, tenderness and violence—the Other can catalyze all these emotions. He or she can also be the focus of our fantasy and imagination, the mirror of our neuroses, and the revealer of our shortcomings. Reassuring or frightening, it is the Other that we seek out, flee from, attempt to seduce, or to destroy—at least symbolically. Without intending it, the Other shatters our limits, our hopes, and the security habits we had been tending so carefully since childhood, influenced by all those stories of heroes and princesses.

Multiplied to the infinity of all our possible and imagined relationships, others become the screen on which we project our dreams of a perfect and ideal life. And then we condemn them, because they turn out to be only human, just like us. We criticize them, because it is easier to see "the speck in our neighbor's eye than the log in our own," as Jesus said. We detest them, because they never live up to our expectations—as if we wanted them to heal our childhood wounds, which is not their job.

Buddhist teachings liken us to "a lotus growing in a pond, whose roots are sunk in the mud. Its flower blooms on the surface in the fullness of day." This fullness of day cannot happen without help from others. In a sense, we are no more than a mosaic of complex influences which are dependent upon shared experience with those who enter and affect our lives.

In all religions it is recommended to imagine ourselves in the place of others, so as to discover new ways of seeing a situation, and so as to understand others instead of destroying them and ourselves. The Buddha said that our enemy is our greatest teacher, from whom we learn patience and forgiveness. He also said that we should consider other beings to have been, at one time or another, our mothers, our fathers, our children. This invites us to recognize a kinship which links us in consciousness with these other parts of ourselves which we experience as separate beings. And this in turn leads us to realize that it is our own attitudes and ways of seeing things which determine what these infinite reflections of ourselves will express.

We each tend to find identity through living in our own world. But awakened beings live in The World. The way to this awakening passes through recognition of the Other. And it also requires accepting responsibility for what we construct, including our mistakes. Other beings offer us the tremendous gift of revealing us to ourselves—and we offer it to them.

Action in the World:
Interdependence and Responsibility

———

Human beings are responsible for most of the problems which are upsetting and destroying the planetary balance. We humans have brought this situation about, and it is up to us to find solutions for it.

🍂

Some of us imagine that it is vain and useless to act in the world, to care about others and try to help them. This attitude is a sign that we have been captured by our own "ego," our self-centeredness. It confines our reality to that of our own narrow, limited world. In this paltry universe every problem becomes an exaggerated source of anxiety. Taking an interest in others seems like an impediment.

If we change our mind and way of seeing things, if we step back and gain some perspective on how we are living, we create a space of freedom in ourselves. Our entire attitude changes. Our daily annoyances seem trivial and insignificant in comparison to far more serious situations lived by persons we know or have heard about. This transformation works progressively on our mental habits, and we discover a tremendous courage in ourselves. From this courage, peace of mind is born.

🍂

———

Time is required in order to develop strength, courage, and inner peace. Do not expect swift and immediate results just because you have decided to change. Your will is not a magic wand of transformation. It is through your every action that this decision becomes effective in your heart.

*

Real changes take place without fanfare. They are a progressive process, not spectacular and sudden. As examples, let us consider two types of change.

The first relates to the philosophy of non-violence. If you are convinced that it is valid, then you will closely observe your own behavior. In the beginning, you will concentrate on your most violent actions, especially if they are physical. Then you will gradually become conscious of your subtler verbal and emotional violence. Little by little, you will gain the ability to prevent any kind of violent action.

The second type of change involves the principle of interdependence. When you understand that your reactions and way of being have many repercussions, you will no longer act in a way that is heedless of others. Then it will be possible for you to examine your reactions in a much vaster perspective, including your social, psychological, and ecological contexts.

*

Insight into the process of interdependence does not come easily to human beings. It contradicts our certainties derived from ego-based experiences. We are used to living and thinking as entities separate from each other and from the world. We believe that objects have a reality of their own. This is reinforced by the experience of possessing things. However, nothing exists in itself, separate from the rest of existence. Everything depends on causes and conditions. As these accumulate and gather momentum, they actualize when the time is ripe, creating the illusion of separate objects.

❧

If we want to become better human beings, we must help others. These two things are inseparable.

❧

Our whole existence bears witness to the relations we establish with others and with the universe. It is the totality of these relations which helps to construct us as we are. This is why our existence expresses in itself all forms of existence.

❧

You are not an entity separate from the rest of the world. The world is you. You are the world.

❧

Your future, your well-being, what will become of you, your peace of mind, and your inner courage—all these are related to others' happiness as well. Your happiness is intimately linked to theirs.

❧

It is not laws that make us into better human beings. Only the transformation of work on our own mind can accomplish this.

❧

The world is a macrocosm of ourselves. Every particle in the universe corresponds to some aspect of our body, and every human being is also an organ or cell in this vast universal body. We each play a specific part which is necessary to the process of the whole. This is why maintaining one's own harmony and balance also means caring for others, without exception.

❧

Everything that happens in the world, even the tiniest drama, sooner or later has an echo in our own existence.

❧

We are all connected, interdependent, and in constant relation. This is why we are responsible for the happiness and unhappiness of all humanity.

❧

Buddhism teaches us to consider everything that happens to us, whether pleasant or unpleasant, as a function of our responsibility. Events arise from our past actions, from imprints left in this life and in previous lives. If we accept this as true, external circumstances become secondary. Priority is given to understanding the causes which have brought about what we are experiencing. Hence it is appropriate to examine the mental and emotional attitudes with which we habitually respond to situations, so as to uncover the mechanisms at work. If we can accomplish this, we will be able to avoid reproducing the conditions which keep these processes going, and ultimately become conscious of their meaning.

❧

The recognition that we are responsible for what we experience offers us a fresh vision of every situation in which we find ourselves. We become free to act in a positive way, transforming our negative habits. Now we know that we have the choice, and that we can do it. This confidence can only be achieved if we stop blaming external circumstances and devote ourselves to understanding and modifying the inner attitudes which have fostered the actualizing of these circumstances.

❧

Reflect upon the connections which bring us together and unite us as human beings. The awareness of our fundamental similarity is a great consolation, for how can we ever feel lonely and isolated again?

❧

Tensions between groups of people can only be resolved through dialogue and non-violence. These alone enable people to face their divergences of opinions and demands, and to find compromises.

❧

Adopting a non-violent attitude does not mean becoming apathetic, nor is it a strategy of escape from confrontation.

Adopting a non-violent attitude means becoming more

responsible. It means caring about the situation at hand.

To live according to this philosophy is to confront oneself, to go to the very heart of the difficulty. It requires taking into account and analyzing all aspects of the problem at hand. The goal is to bring divergent points of view closer together, to find solutions which are acceptable to all parties involved in the conflict.

❧

Lack of respect for oneself and for others leads to extreme forms of violence. Disrespect is a sign of ignorance of others and of life. Intolerance, disrespect, and aggression are all on the rise, for they are closely linked with each other.

❧

If we could all understand the importance of respect, it would greatly reduce our violent impulses, and war would lose its foundations.

❧

What you do and what you are, including your spiritual evolution, depends on others. If you realize this, responding to their needs is no longer a burden, but a spontaneous and necessary act.

❧

The world is growing smaller. We are more and more dependent upon each other. Politics and conflicts demonstrate this, as do economic and ecological imbalances, as well as scientific advances.

❧

If your desire to help others is based on a motivation which is unselfish and untainted by desire for personal power, and if you have the capacity for it, then engaging in politics can be a positive thing. Working for the good of others becomes your priority. This priority will develop a courage and determination which will help you to bring about real changes in the heart of society.

❧

Achieving peace in the outer world requires working first on oneself to achieve inner peace.

❧

Non-violence is a specifically human attitude, based on dialogue. It is also based on knowledge and understanding of the other. It requires accepting differences—in other words, tolerance and mutual respect. It is motivated by a spirit of openness and reconciliation.

❧

If helping others seems too difficult for you, then at least try not to harm them.

❧

It is only human to try to escape our responsibilities. It is all to easy to blame external causes and persons for our problems. This is escapism. If you can be honest and impartial, you will see through this. Peace of mind is destroyed by denying the reality of phenomena. Such lack of courage will gradually wear you down inside. But acceptance of your responsibility will help you to develop serenity, peace, and self-confidence.

❧

Analysis of our own past helps to understand our present reactions. Situating others in the context of their past teaches tolerance.

❧

Devoting oneself to the goal of world peace must begin with an immense caring, and a real love for all. This peace can never be accomplished in a context of racial, cultural, or religious intolerance. It requires a recognition of the fundamental unity of human beings, despite their apparent diversity.

❧

If you are confronted with relationship problems, you should look at the real nature of the relations you maintain. Some friendships are founded on worldly success, immature emotions, family ties, or on economic interests. These are unstable relationships. They are fed by relations of dependency which will drop by the wayside in the course of events and of your own evolution.

A true and deep friendship is not based on power over another. It never fosters dependency. True friendship means sharing, selfless giving, communication, authenticity, and acceptance of the other. Nothing can affect or destroy such a friendship.

❧

Do not run from your problems. It is essential to face them. This enables you to see them clearly as they are. Then you can analyze them, get a grip on them, and solve them.

In order to win any battle, you need a good strategy.

Knowing the enemy's strength and resources is fundamental.

Victory over the difficulties we encounter means we must observe their every aspect, neglecting nothing.

❧

Do not waste precious time. Every second counts, for every second is unique, irreplaceable, and filled with incredible possibilities.

We squander our time like spoiled children who think they will live forever. We always put off till tomorrow what we can do today. We throw away many possibilities for action, happiness, and making others happy.

How can you be so sure that you will be alive tomorrow? Reflect upon the meaning of your life now. Reality is in the present, and it is vain to live in hopes for the future. Do not harm others, show them love, let them into your life now.

❧

Constantly practice seeing others in a positive light. This will establish a feeling of affinity. You will no longer be concerned about others' opinions of you, nor will you fear their judgment or rejection. This will eliminate the need to equivocate to yourself and to others so as to protect yourself. By accepting yourself as you are, you will be deeply accepted by those around you. You will never again be prone to loneliness or depression.

❧

Always waiting for others to take the first step means thinking yourself superior to them. This creates a barrier in your relationships. If indulged in, it will isolate you more and more from those around you.

❧

Whatever the situation, whether you are right or wrong, practice compassion, understanding, and generosity.

❧

Dialogue is a source of happiness.

❧

Always put yourself in the other's place. Suspend your own opinions and judgments for a moment, so as to understand their point of view. Many conflicts can be avoided in this way.

❧

Our fundamental nature is good and kind. But believing this is not enough to transform us. We must change our perception of ourselves, so as to be more open to others, and to develop our ability to act with them in harmony with this fundamental nature.

❧

Adopt the same attitude toward all human beings. Your fundamental duty and responsibility to a beggar are the same as to the president of a country.

❧

If the person you are talking to does not agree with your ideas, and if this person is unreceptive and unwilling to change, then do not attempt to impose your knowledge.

❧

When conflict occurs, establish a dialogue whenever possible. Talk, and keep talking, until solutions begin to appear.

❧

Live in service to the world.

❧

Our only real power is in helping others.

❧

In a moment of conflict, violence might seem to be a powerful remedy. But this blinds you to its later negative consequences. Always consider the consequences of your decisions.

❧

Times change. Living realistically means living in one's time. For example, as a religious leader, I must work to find ways to adapt our traditions to everyday life as it is. It is imperative that certain spiritual teachings become more accessible to people. Then they can choose what is most appropriate for them.

❧

We reject others' criticisms of us, yet feel we have the right to criticize them. And we rarely come to their defense when they are criticized.

❧

Leaving victory to the other, even to an enemy, is not a sign of failure. Patience is not a sign of weakness, but of real courage and inner strength.

❧

The intention to do harm is not part of any being's fundamental nature. But people do become victims and slaves of their own emotions. They are dominated and manipulated by external events and circumstances. This is why it is useless and immature to indulge in resentment or anger with them.

❧

Do not hate those who destroy sacred sites and monasteries, for they do it out of ignorance. The Buddha himself did not become distraught by this type of violation.

❧

Taking satisfaction from an enemy's misfortune and despair, feeling vindicated for the wrong that was done to you, will never bring you happiness.

❧

Ordinary beings are dominated by their passions, and their emotions tend to be extreme. We cannot help them if we behave as they do. Yet if we show ourselves to be too different from them, they may reject us, and become totally confused. They would have liked to see us as a friend, but see us instead as an enemy, because our reactions are too different.

❧

Some people love you, others hate you. Their feelings may have little or relation to your behavior. Sometimes their reactions have good reasons, sometimes no reasons. Do not be attached to any of this, and give without calculation. And be attentive of their needs.

❧

The pain we experience always seems wrong, often intolerable. No one else can feel it the way we do. The same thing applies to others. We are strangers to what they experience, and we do not understand them.

❧

Our indifference to others is the source of many forms of suffering.

❧

We must transform our mind so that it becomes natural for us to help and protect others. This should be our first priority.

❧

Our greatest enemy is our insane narcissistic love. This is what separates us from others.

❧

Putting yourself in another's place makes you aware of your own self-centered tendencies. Then you free yourself from this "ego" which is the source of so much suffering.

❧

It is essential to become kind and generous. Then we can act in a truly positive way with others, and are able to participate in the harmony of the universe.

❧

We must place all our abilities in service to the world and to others.

Education

Education helps people to understand and choose what will bring them knowledge and happiness. It also exposes the causes of suffering. This is why education must be a fundamental value in human life.

❧

Contemporary society sees education only as a means of producing people who can compete and succeed in gaining power and recognition. True education is a learning process which helps individuals to develop their inner qualities and allow their basic human nature to flourish.

❧

The current social order fosters fear, anxiety, doubt, and constant stress. In spite of this, it is possible to nurture positive human qualities during childhood. This is the task of education.

❧

Children should live only in a positive atmosphere, so as not to encourage their negative tendencies.

❧

Parents and children now choose more and more often to live separately. Family solidarity is diminishing. Respect and love are also on the wane. All of these are reflections of the loss of meaning which our societies are undergoing.

❧

Education is not spontaneous. It requires that principles be practiced and repeated over years. This is the only way we achieve transformation. This kind of learning process is vital if individuals are to live in community and become better human beings.

❧

The younger generations are constantly barraged with bad news, full of violence. They are thoroughly and unrelentingly immersed in fear and tension in the media. This is the first time in human history that such a phenomenon has occurred on this scale. We must reflect on the effects of modern life upon our children.

❧

Education has advanced everywhere in the world. However, instead of instilling kindness and happiness in people, it has often created suffering, dissatisfaction, and frustration.

❧

The first thing education should teach children is how dependent we all are on each other.

❧

Through images broadcast on television, children discover a virtual world, based on violence. This world is not reality. It represents only an infinitesimal part of existence. Yet they identify with it.

4

DEATH

For most of us, the cycle of births and deaths is involuntary. Only beings who have developed a tremendous capability of compassion can choose to be reborn in a certain form so as to pursue their mission of helping others to be free of the hellish realms ruled by the darkness of ego. Death is a temporary escape from these relentless cycles. It is a key moment, and a privileged and decisive one. Those whose vision of life is vast enough to include many births and deaths prepare for this passage so as achieve less and less tormented incarnations. Those who have fully lived their life in this particular body realize the importance of dying in peace and with no regrets. They are certain of having "succeeded" in human life—in other words, of having "received all I had to receive, given all I had to give, and done all I had to do," in the words of Swami Prajnanpad, a great Indian scholar and spiritual teacher.

The meaning of our life depends on our awareness of this "other side of the mirror," this implacable and unavoidable transition. It depends on how deeply conscious we are of this unpredictable moment, lasting only an instant, time enough for one final, unique breath. The body returns to its elements. The spirit leaves for a voyage into the unknown.

Death and its process are at the heart of Buddhist teaching and practice. Life is but a preparation for this vertiginous, absolute letting-go. None of us can escape this dissolution of all our sensations and concepts. Only spirit accompanies our awareness beyond this fascinating and terrifying frontier. Spirit guides mind. The forms that appear in our mind, the fears that it arouses, the stillness and confidence that underlie it, the peace which calms it, the terrors which seize and overthrow it, all depend on us. Everything depends on the qualities of transformation and self-mastery we have developed. Learning generosity, detachment from one's possessions, and living in harmony with being, all help to facilitate this irreversible transition. Fears of death, of abandoning possessions and loved ones, become as tenuous as the very air of that last breath before this body is abandoned forever.

It is essential to prepare ourselves for death. To help others around us to die is also essential. Last regrets can twist hearts and bodies. The urgency of imminent death demands the gift of total and unconditional love. It is crucial at these moments to offer forgiveness, a smile, and words whose perfume and beauty comfort and caress the dying one like a necklace of flowers. We are called to calm, console, reassure, love—whether with a simple stroking of the hand, or with a deep looking into their eyes. We must accept their death and this seeming abandonment so as to allow them their freedom. The freedom to die consciously, reconciled with oneself and with others. No turning back. Neither for ourselves, nor for the one who is embarking into this invisible elsewhere.

Preparation for Death

————

Reflect upon the many and varied aspects of impermanence. You will observe that nothing lasts, nothing is ultimately stable. Your beliefs, emotions, feelings for others, possessions, and future projects—all these can change and vanish in an instant. Everything is always evolving, regardless of your desires and strategies. The latter may include all sorts of ways of reassuring yourself in the illusory belief that you really do possess something or someone, or that your life really is permanent. But everything is bound to disappear, including you. And at the moment of death, you will be alone in crossing this threshold. Reflect upon the many and varied aspects of impermanence, with no evasion or masking of this last moment. In this way you can learn to live each moment fully, as if it were the last. Then most of your supposed options will seem trivial, for you will go to the essence of things. This is the only way you can learn detachment and the true value of beings, things, and your own actions.

❧

It is better to die, even today, than to continue to lead a life of luxury based on ill-gotten gains.

❧

————

All that you do, say, and think, what you give, the way you transform your mind and life—all of this works to create favorable rebirths.

❧

No one can claim to know that they will still be alive at the end of the day. We must be prepared to die at any time. And we must be prepared to see those we love die at any time. Only in this way can our attitude change.

❧

Never suppose that it is useless to prepare yourself to die at any time. For even if we live for many more years, we can never be totally ready to confront this passage. However, it is otherwise with fully awakened beings.

❧

We waste and spoil our lives by our frequent indulgence in futile diversions. We do not understand the truth of impermanence. We fail to see how this principle applies to our own life. And when old age arrives, we are left with only our regrets to face the accelerating flight of time, which has left us behind with no respite.

❧

A spiritual practice whose worldview includes a limitless number of rebirths, and a multidimensional time which confounds our habitual concepts, puts death in a very different, vaster perspective. Death is no longer such a terrible and categorical finality. It is only a term, no longer a marker of final and total annihilation of a human life. Death takes its place as one of the moments in a vaster existence, stretching over an immensity of cycles of multidimensional time. In this context, the instant when one leaves the body is no more than a change of clothes: worn-out clothes, bearing the marks of the aging of our particular organism. We leave it, trade it for another, and our spiritual evolution goes on.

❧

It is essential to meditate on the process of death in such a way as to deepen our insight into the nature of mind.

❧

We must prepare for old age and the moment of death. Otherwise, when these circumstances come upon us, the psychological and emotional shock will be so intense that we will be utterly lost and bewildered. Meditate on the meaning of old age, meditate on the meaning of death, and also on the meaning of your trials. This will show you the meaning of your life. You will become stronger, more courageous, and determined to change. To anticipate such meanings will help you to find a great calm, an immense peace, and an absolute confidence. These will be of priceless value when you do arrive at these passages.

❧

From the first instant of your conception until your last breath, you are accompanied and sustained by the love and affection of other beings.

✿

Whatever tradition you espouse, if the notion of life beyond death is meaningless for you, and yet you are committed to doing good, then you will surely have fewer regrets at the moment of death. On the other hand, if you have a religious view of death as a real and important passage, and yet have not yet engaged in a spiritual practice for lack of time, then begin right now to do everything in your power to prepare for it. Later will be too late.

✿

Most people reject the concept of reincarnation, often through ignorance of what it really means. Yet this rejection poses a number of problems, such as how to explain and understand injustice. Buddhism advocates a pragmatic approach. There are certainly real phenomena which are not accessible to our direct perception. In such cases, always use your powers of reason, deductive logic, and analysis. If evidence begins to accumulate in favor of such a phenomenon, it is legitimate to conclude that it is at least a real possibility. Now, apply this method to the hypothesis of rebirths. Most of us do not remember our previous lives. Yet some people do have such memories, and have provided evidence through their words and experiences that these memories are authentic.

✿

A form of consciousness is transmitted from one incarnation to another. The total number of rebirths is limitless. Some of them take place in the human realm. Others happen in different realms, which we experience according to the law of karma—in other words, causality. Rebirth is inevitable. But rebirth as a human being is a privilege. It is the only state which offers us the possibility of realizing awakening. If you think about the sufferings which you have already undergone, and imagine that you will have to repeat these in a thousand more cycles of existence, then you will waste no time in putting an end to this process, if there is the slightest chance of it. Practice with the aim of freeing yourself from this chain.

❧

Recognizing the true urgency of engaging in a spiritual path implies a constant awareness of death. Far from being morbid, this awareness gives life a unique flavor and fills your practice with amazing strength and substance.

❧

Every instant is unique. Live it fully.

The Moment of Death

———

In the moment of the last breath, the grosser forms of awareness disappear. These are the foundations of illusions and of sensory perception. Externally, life comes to an end. Internally, this is far from the case. Life continues: a subtle state of consciousness remains. This subtle consciousness is the fundamental nature of mind. It is free of all attachment and emotion. It is free of ego.

❧

Even if our existence has been in vain, filled with negative emotions, when the moment of death arrives we still have one more chance to act, at least to some extent, upon what we have been. This last opportunity reflects the power of repentance. This power arises from our consciousness of our errors, and from our total certainty that the imprints left by our actions, thoughts, and deeds will persist and will influence our further becoming. In this case, we must make one final and total effort to transform ourselves. This force of repentance—if it is strong and sincere—will then permeate us and have an effect on the unfavorable causes and conditions which we have created.

❧

Scientific beliefs differ from those of Buddhism regarding the reality of death. Science maintains that when breathing ends and the heart stops beating, clinical brain-death occurs only moments later. Thus all outer signs of life have disappeared. But Buddhist teaching claims that there are four important stages which follow this physiological process. These are invisible to the eye of an external observer, and unmeasurable by current medical instruments. But they are real events in an inner process which has been perceived and described by masters in the Tibetan tradition. This process is the dissolution of gross forms of consciousness associated with the senses. Each phase of it is symbolically represented by a specific color.

First come the white, red, and black phases, in that order. The fourth phase is experienced by the subject as a kind of infinite, luminous space. It has been characterized as the space of the Clear Light. It corresponds to the fundamental nature of mind and spirit, to that subtle consciousness that reincarnates in birth after birth.

🖌

The positive motivation which we retain at the time of dying helps our passage through the stages between death and the next birth. If our daily practice has prepared us for it, then we can spontaneously call upon this motivation whenever we need it, remembering that we can and should use this resource to open our awareness so that it can act effectively.

🖌

All perpetuity is illusory. Impermanence is the law of existence. We are like children who cannot part with our toys. We act as if our carefree times will last forever. When we grow up, we see that everything is slipping through our hands. Yet we mask this reality, thinking that denial will somehow enable us to keep a hold on beings and things. The moment of death is the ultimate moment of truth. Manipulation of self and others is no longer possible. Lying to oneself now reveals itself as a hindrance. Nothing can mask this reality of impermanence any more. It has implacably caught up with us.

🖌

Death is simply a passage. It marks the transition from one state to another. During this transformation everything is forever being destroyed and recreated.

❧

The state of mind in which we die determines the conditions of our rebirth.

❧

The fullness of serenity and peace which we experience at the moment of death depends on the meaning we have given to our life. The regrets we experience are a reflection of what we have made of our life.

❧

The accumulation of negative actions during our life generates a tremendous fear at the moment of death. Terrifying visions arise in our mind. They remind us that our human potential has not been well used. No respite is offered us during this final moment. Memory preserves the record of what we have done, and what we have been. It overwhelms us and leaves us desperate and confused.

❧

It is indispensable for both the dying person and those who are in contact with them to accept the reality of death. This acceptance gives the person the right to abandon their bodily envelope in peace and without fear. It offers them the freedom to die without regrets, and to abandon their last earthly ties. For loved ones, this letting-go means not resisting the subtle awareness of death, not obliging the dying person to remain invisibly behind in this physical realm. It means freeing oneself from the selfish aspect of loss, so as to give to the departing one the possibility of experiencing fully the stages which will lead them to one world or another. In this context, it is of little importance whether one believes in an afterlife or not. What is important is total affection, and a peaceful atmosphere — a final gift and proof of unconditional love. Is this not a wonderful offering ?

❧

Helping someone to be born and helping someone to die are the two most important, most essential, most extraordinary human actions we are ever called upon to perform.

❧

Westerners are afraid of death, and hide it. This is a mistake. How can we ever understand the meaning of life if we conceal this reality?

❧

Birth is an important moment. But during our own birth, we have no power to affect things which have already been decided. For example, we must accept our sex or country of birth as they are. On the other hand, although our death is just as inevitable, and just as imposed upon us by circumstances, we can have an influence during its process — and thereby influence our future births. We are responsible for our becoming.

5

MIND

For over 2,500 years, the goal of various meditation techniques transmitted from teacher to disciple has been to harmonize mind and body. The aim is a fully incarnated spirit, a mind which no longer functions like a parasite which misleads, drains, and often fatigues its host's vital system with induced illnesses. The inter-dependence which links everything in the cosmos also applies to our own mind-body system. Spirit needs a body in order to expe-rience its center through certain forms of consciousness. From there it can radiate, grow, participate in the world, and find its true place. The universe is reflected in us. Even physically, we are its echo. As sparks of the whole cosmos, we are all linked together.

Buddhism is above all pragmatic. Phenomena are neither independent nor permanent, they have no existence in them-selves, and are illusory. Analyzing them by taking both mind and body fully into account enables us to act in accordance with the truth of the impermanence of all objects and sensations. In the desert, you may believe in the reality of a mirage until you get close enough to it. The same thing applies to phenomena which seem so solid and fixed. Only a penetrating observation can ver-ify that they are appearances derived from a chain of causes and effects. They are each imbedded in an insubstantial continuity which was one thing in the past, something different now, and will be something else again in the future. Behind the appearances, this continuity contains no self-existent identity whatsoever.

Inanimate objects, even the cycle of this entire universe, all participate in a single continuum of transformation of matter, which includes our own human bodies.

Mind has its own continuum with qualities specific to it, though mind and body interact with each other on a number of levels. Certain forms of consciousness which compose it are dependent on the body, especially those associated with the senses. Masters have described their experiences of a more subtle level of consciousness, developed through dream and meditation techniques. This level is the very foundation of mind and spirit, and is sometimes referred to in conceptual terms as wisdom and knowledge. It is this nature that transmigrates from one life to another, carrying along the imprints we have left on other forms of consciousness. It is thanks to this fundamental nature that we can someday, like the Buddha, have access to absolute Knowledge.

Mind, Spirit, and Emotions

It is an error to accept negative emotions as if they were basic components of mind. They are not fundamental to our nature. If they were, it would be impossible to overcome them, and this is not the case. We have the ability and the choice to free ourselves from them. Failure to reflect deeply upon them indicates a lack of mindfulness. Then they invade us, blinding us and leading us to react without discrimination. We give in to them, and this submission even seems natural. But the deeper nature of mind is one of love and compassion. Expansion of this nature directly dissipates the hypnotic power of negative states of mind.

❧

We deny the destructive impact of our fits of anger by justifying them. We claim that it is natural and appropriate to respond in this way to injustices committed against us, and that this also applies to injustices in the world. But we are being manipulated by ego. It draws us into reaction, and obscures our true freedom of action. It discharges us from all responsibility by making us believe that our life requires this kind of emotional excitement.

❧

Ignorance, craving, and aversion are the primary poisons of the mind. Ignorance is the foundation of all negative emotion. Craving and aversion are its followers. Ignorance employs aversion and its corollaries, anger and hatred, to create enemies with whom the ego can engage in battle. It manipulates craving and its partner, attachment, so as to strengthen their rule over events, beings, and objects. The only outcome of ignorance is to reinforce the power of ego. Any means will do to attain this.

❧

Diminishing our selfishness requires loving others, and concentrating only on their positive qualities.

❦

Spirit is our inner master. It can express itself by guiding us, transforming our behavior, and outlook on life. To let it be means to surrender to this inner master always, at every moment of our daily life.

❦

Emotional illusion is an agitation of mind which destroys our peace, happiness, serenity, and power of compassion.

❦

Discipline is the only means by which we can conquer and channel our illusions. Without discipline these illusions grow larger, overpowering us and creating unfavorable causes and conditions for our present and future existences.

❦

The worst power of illusion is its denigration of the mind's positive qualities and its justification of the mind's flaws. Illusion reinforces acquired negative emotions in us as if they were permanent features of our mind. Then they begin to seem overwhelming and insurmountable. Yet in reality they are nothing but phantom constructions elaborated by our senses. Insight into the reality behind our illusions gives us the energy and lucidity needed to transform them.

❦

Negative emotions and positive spiritual qualities function like locks in a canal: when the level is lowered in one, it is raised in the other.

🍂

Light banishes darkness. Heat drives away cold. And positive qualities of mind prevent negative ones from manifesting.

🍂

Spiritual practice strengthens mental stability. It should be a source of joy. A practice that is too fatiguing can turn out to be harmful. Rest when your reserves are low. Too much pressure results in the opposite of what you are aiming for. It creates a breach in your exhausted psyche, a space where negative emotions can take you by surprise.

🍂

The spirit of enlightenment consists of doing everything to help others to be free of suffering and its causes. It has nothing to do with emotion or sentimentality about their circumstances. It is a natural force, based on a strong will and an immense determination. This spiritual capacity is serene, stable, unshakable. It is never fully acquired, yet it can be gradually learned.

🍂

The transformation of mind cannot be based on mere intellectual knowledge. It demands a discipline and a practice. These are indispensable conditions for transformation leading to inner peace.

❧

Craving, aversion, arrogance, hatred, lust, anger, and attachment are some of the various manifestations of the ego and expressions of the "I."

❧

Let go of your judgments and your critical mind. You do not know the real motivations of other beings, or their real past. So what do you know about them now? Why be so attached to outer manifestations? Accept beings as they are, and love them. Rejecting them will not help them to change. However, the love and confidence you express can work miracles.

❧

Negative states of mind destroy balance and harmony in both mind and body. They affect you first and foremost, and then others—especially when you resort to hurtful, aggressive, and violent words and actions. These states of mind affect your own inner peace and that of others around you. This sets in motion a vicious circle of action and reaction. Do not let this dominate your life.

❧

What does it matter how others see us? What real value do fame and social recognition have? If our attitude is sound, then these things have no importance for this life or for future lives. On the other hand, never overlook the unfavorable psychic impact of imprints left by your negative actions. These imprints have a definite influence on your evolution and your happiness.

⚘

A calm and serene mind is relaxed, happy, peaceful, and spacious. An agitated mind creates stress in the physical and psychic organism. Opening our hearts and minds has a freeing action on emotions such as fear, anxiety, and worry.

⚘

A well-disciplined mind generates healthy and just actions. An undisciplined, negative, and selfish mind generates unhealthy and unjust actions.

⚘

Discipline of the mind implies a taming of one's thoughts, emotions, and actions.

⚘

Our mind is the axis of our life. When it succumbs to negative influences, this exponentially increases our unconscious rebirths. But when mastered, it frees us from these relentless cycles.

⚘

Work on negative emotions is a long-term process. Perseverance, will, and determination are necessary. When you become discouraged, when your progress seems insignificant, read or meditate on the lives of great masters of the past, such as the

Buddha. All of them had to go through difficulties and often incredible sufferings in their spiritual quest. It takes great courage to realize oneself and the Way.

❧

The belief that mastery of the mind can be rapidly attained is a sign of tremendous arrogance.

❧

Anger is an obstruction in our spiritual evolution. One moment of indulgence in anger can destroy the hard work of years, even lifetimes. Anger is one of the most terrible enemies of spirituality.

❧

The compassion of the Buddhas is a kind of feeling, but one which is free from the negative imprints of ego.

❧

No one can pretend that they have never felt emotions such as resentment, hatred, craving, pride, and aversion. Examine your mind with honesty. You will observe that these emotions often arise without any real external impetus. They break out spontaneously, through habit. If you change your automatic habits of thought and action, you will find that these states will naturally die away.

❧

All bad habits can be purified by the power of repentance.

❧

Repentance is a tremendous force. It alone can counteract the destructive power of our negative thoughts and emotions. Never underestimate the mind's potential to create disorder. It beguiles us into acting out our impulses, as if we were caught up in an avalanche, whose cold congeals and desensitizes us spiritually. Then we are trapped in the snow of our illusions.

❧

Our bad habits are built up over numerous lifetimes. Their roots are deep. And our "virtuous" practices are relatively recent in comparison—these are more like young sprouts, easy to uproot. Be mindful of your true potential, advance upon the Way one step at a time, and never give into the temptation to believe that there is a quick and easy way. Then you will accomplish work on yourself which brings gradual, but profound stability.

In order for a seed to be transformed into a flower, it must receive the necessary nutrients at the appropriate time and season. Our mind works the same way.

❧

Meditation, analysis, and visualization of the positive qualities of mind will not suffice to change our habits if they are only practiced sporadically.

❧

Every being we meet, and every situation we encounter, should incite us to exchange our negative habits for positive actions.

———

❧

The continuity of consciousness accompanies us from life to life. Favorable and unfavorable imprints are accumulated and deposited in the continuum of consciousness during these existences. Neither wholesome nor destructive imprints can have the slightest effect on the natural, fundamental state of spirit. Nevertheless, these causes, effects, and conditions are transmitted from rebirth to rebirth until they reach their term. Subtle and gross levels of mind function in a complementary way during our incarnations. Do not neglect your practice. Be very determined to transform yourself so as to change the course of your existences and diminish the impact of previous accumulations.

❧

The notion that wandering spirits or souls intrude in our lives so as to prevent us from evolving spiritually is a mistake, and a manipulation by the ego. The real obstacles we encounter originate in our own mind. We are responsible.

❧

Our spiritual efforts cleanse our mind of negative imprints accumulated in other lifetimes.

❧

Only spirit can purify spirit.

❧

Buddhism is a science of spirit. We are the material in which spirit works.

❧

Buddhism gives priority to human development over transcendental states of consciousness. It would be unrealistic to strive for access to higher planes while our own capacity to be fully human is stunted.

❧

Every negative emotion has a specific antidote. The effectiveness of these antidotes depends on our mindfulness and will to apply them.

❧

Our enemies only act against us during this life, but our negative emotions devour our minds during other existences.

❧

Our extreme emotions are never our friends or allies. To entertain and cherish them only leads to an increase in their intensity and power over us.

❧

A negative emotion which has been destroyed through transformation cannot sprout up again. This is quite different from our physical enemies, who may disappear for awhile, regaining force, and attack again. Once a negative emotion has really lost its harbor in our mind, there is no doorway by which it can return. Although the power of these mental states is not fundamentally real, they will persist as long as we have not fully confronted and channeled them until the end of their resistance.

§

All phenomena and all emotions are dreamlike and illusory. They bear witness to our ignorance and confusion.

§

Insight into the true nature of emotions gives us the means to transform them.

§

If we are mindful, we will foresee the consequences of our acts, our words, and our thoughts. This awareness enables us to apply the right antidote when necessary, and to work progressively on the prior motivations which create psychological habits.

§

To remain a slave of one's emotions, believing it impossible to master them and our own mind, is the sign of a lack of courage and willpower.

§

Our past suffering works like a distorting lens upon our mind. Letting go of all attachment to details of such memories shatters this lens. And our mind becomes vast and luminous.

§

Any situation or event can include good and bad aspects. If you concentrate your attention on the good ones, you will observe that your overall feeling is agreeable and positive. Everything depends on the attitude you adopt. Your responsibility consists of choosing one or another of these perspectives. This choice will determine your becoming and that of the world in which you evolve.

❧

A feeling can be negative, positive, or neutral. A Buddha is able to experience feelings, but their qualities are radically different from those experienced by "ordinary" beings.

❧

Our reality is transformed in proportion to our actions or our illusions.

❧

Inner experience has a greater impact than outer experience. The transformation of our mind depends on it.

❧

If our psychic life is positive and constructive, the difficulties we face will seem relatively light. But if it is pessimistic, then obstacles and conflicts will appear everywhere.

❧

A mind ruled by anger cannot distinguish good from evil. Like fire and water, wisdom and violence are incompatible. Anger is one of the fundamental evils in our societies.

❧

All that we are arises from and depends on spirit.

❧

Meditation involves training the mind. It is useful for everyone, no matter what their beliefs or tradition.

❧

Analytical contemplation is of fundamental importance. It develops our discrimination, our mindfulness, and our lucidity.

❧

It is necessary to combine analytical contemplation with mental concentration on a specific object, so as to develop both inner calm and the ability to discriminate.

❧

Human beings are responsible for what they are. Only they can master their own minds. Buddhism offers many techniques for helping people to attain this power over themselves.

❧

In addition to specific antidotes for particular negative emotions, there is a general antidote for all such mental states: seeing and recognizing the true nature of phenomena.

❧

From the beginning, the Buddha realized how difficult it is to unmask the constructs of the unconscious mind. These thoughts and emotions are dangerous because they are so entrenched and disguised, and we do not see them operating. They are like a volcano which is going to erupt someday. When that day arrives it will be too late to avoid catastrophe, because we have waited too long, refusing to acknowledge and examine these phenomena. Mastery of the mind must include a thorough and comprehensive knowledge of who we really are. Otherwise we are like agitated sleepers, tormented by nightmares which we are powerless to end, because we have no knowledge of their true nature and causes.

❧

Our best interests and our future are linked with those of others. We must see ourselves as connected to the rest of the universe, to humans, animals, all forms of life. We must stop living as separate beings, an ego among other egos.

❧

My task is to serve others.

❧

Our mind is like an agitated monkey locked in an empty house. We perceive the world in a fragmented way. Our perceptions depend on our sensory organs, and we jump from one to the other without taking the time to question and analyze the sensations we experience. And we act without any inkling of the consequences of this agitation.

❧

The true nature of mind is luminous spirit. It is independent of all forms, sensations, feelings, or colors. It is indefinable, because it is beyond any measurement or concept.

❧

Working on illusions means working on mind.

❧

Ever since it began, Buddhism has known about the unconscious mind. But our methods do not include forms of therapy such as Western psychoanalysis. It is an interesting technique, but it applies to a different cultural context.

❧

Certain levels of consciousness and the thoughts which emanate from them are closely linked to the brain and its physiological activity. These phenomena change in relation to molecular changes. But this does not apply to the highest and most subtle level of consciousness, which is independent of any physical support.

❧

Buddhist tradition describes thousands of processes and states of the psyche. It would take many lifetimes to know and understand them all.

❧

The destiny of this world and of the entire universe follows the destiny of spirit.

Mind and Body

Mind dominates body. Our way of thinking influences all the organism's sensations. A painful feeling may be experienced as less or more intense according to our state of mind.

❧

That which is beneficial for me and my body also helps others.

❧

Every action which helps others increases your own spiritual strength.

❧

When your body becomes ill because of your own neglect, it is better to make sure you have a regular, healthy diet than to pray for healing.

❧

When you fall ill, it is easy to blame it on microbes. A little reflection shows that the state of your body must have favored the development of these germs. When your organism is balanced and healthy, such symptoms do not occur. The same is true of the mind. We also tend to try to evade responsibility in this domain, and we are constantly supported in this by outer influences. Instead of complaining, why not do something about it? Then you will stop catering to your own weakness and lack of resolve to live your own life.

❧

Being rich and powerful is not a problem in itself. It can be beneficial if our motivation is pure, and if we dedicate ourselves to serving others.

❧

From a Buddhist point of view, there is no such thing as a permanent, autonomous, eternal entity. There is no separate and independent "soul" such as is spoken of in some religious traditions. The fundamental nature of spirit and of the mind/body relationship has no relation to any concept which relies on "eternalist" assumptions.

❧

The experience of "ordinary" consciousness depends on sensations and perceptions elicited by a given object. This experience is not the same as that of our fundamental consciousness. The latter is pure knowledge, unconditioned by concepts, memories, events in space-time, and any system relating to the body.

❧

The body is the abode of the mind, and it should be at home there. But the mind of most human beings is always wandering away. Criticizing, judging, seeking pleasure and sensual satisfaction, the mind becomes lost in its parallel universes. It is like an unlucky burglar who only finds houses empty of valuable possessions. Our responsibility is to bring the wandering mind back to its home in our inner being. Only then can it correctly evaluate the world around it, and act appropriately.

❧

To live in the present moment means not allowing ourselves to be distracted by our sensations, our regrets, desires, or projects. Our thoughts then become like ocean tides which come and go. We are not attached to these waves. We are free. Then peace unfolds within us.

❧

The mind becomes attached to sensory experiences. By habit, it identifies its own existence with these illusory sensations. But the true nature of mind is spirit, free of these mental creations and of physical perceptions.

❧

Compassion and humor act directly on the body, increasing its well-being and balance. Conversely, unhealthy attitudes disturb the body. The body/mind relationship affords ample proof that human health depends on positive feelings.

Mind, Spirit, and Buddha-nature

If ignorance were inherent in the fundamental nature of mind, no human being would have ever awakened to the truth.

❧

Self-confidence is fundamental. It enables us to be fully aware of our human potential. This potential has been described as Buddha-nature, the Clear Light of the spirit—our essential nature.

❧

Our mind often leads us to believe that the phenomena and events we experience are either pure or impure. These judgments are based on fear. But our judgments and fears, our categories of pure and impure, originate in us, not in the objects of our experience. They are a trap of the ego, which thereby catches us and enslaves us. But if we analyze these various categories from the perspective of the true spiritual nature of mind, we will find that they have no underlying reality.

❧

The Clear Light of the spirit is continuously present. It is revealed between each moment of conceptual thought.

❧

Only when you consent to free yourself from your concepts will you have access to spirit, the fundamental nature of mind.

§

All beings have Buddha-nature.

§

The fundamental nature of mind is neutral. This is why it is possible to purify it of all harmful imprints.

§

All negative mental states come to an end.

§

The spirit of Buddha, the subtle mind, the Clear Light, our primordial nature ... it is without beginning or end, and independent of any physical support.

§

Nirvana is a particular quality of spirit.

6

ETHICS AND SCIENCE

Ethics

———

In the future (which has already arrived) we will be facing increasing problems related to biological cloning of plants, animals, and even human beings. We must also face the implications of "eugenic" technology, which uses embryonic screening, making it possible over years to design a new genetic heritage. The catastrophic results of our other mass technological applications are already upon us: the hole in the ozone layer, and global warming.

We must also take into account the growing chasm between rich and poor, manifested geographically as the imbalance between North and South, which considers the sufferings of poorer countries as of less importance than those of richer ones.

As has often been noted, we human beings are our own worst predators. In the fields of politics, economics, genetic engineering, bioethics, human rights, and religion, we now exercise a wide variety of powerful tools, vastly increasing the range of expression of everything we are, and vividly recalling the myth

———

of the sorcerer's apprentice. Meanwhile, our ancient repressed demons threatened to return, and we seem oblivious to the fact that our policies are robbing future generations of their prospects.

This context explains the priority the Dalai Lama has given in recent years to ethics and their relation to behavior. At this juncture of the third millennium, he maintains that "A revolution is necessary. A spiritual revolution founded upon universal ethical principles based on international consensus." This hope is based on several observations.

First, our responsibility for wars and ecological disturbances is now undeniable. These have their origins in human unconsciousness and selfishness. It is the duty of human beings to correct what they have done. This duty affects the future of humanity.

Whatever our culture, our religion, or the country we live in, we are all united by the desire to find happiness and end suffering. This necessity can form a basis for constructing a new planetary ethics. Globalization and new developments in economics, politics, and science demonstrate more than ever that we are all connected and interdependent. These interconnections impose upon us the obligation to establish and follow ethical principles based on the fundamental things we have in common, rather than upon cultural or religious particularities.

If it is true, as the Buddha said, that we are what we think, and that each of our thoughts influences the world, then our own part in this responsibility compels us to begin now to see ourselves differently, as existing in a global and interactive context. This is urgent, for our planet is sick, and its symptoms are increasing and developing in our physical and psychic environments. The treatment which can cure the majority of these illnesses relates to human nature as much as to the universe in general. The symptoms—which reflect our social disturbances—are afflicting the whole Earth, and their deep treatment must be one which works upon the human psyche. We are all involved in this.

Ethical Behavior

The foundation of ethical discipline is the desire to help others.

❧

A universal ethics of behavior will require us to collect and develop a humanistic information base. This information must take into account the problems of all beings, so as to find overall solutions which everyone can apply, whatever the traditions, religions, cultures, or current politics in the countries involved.

❧

If we are to establish a universal ethical discipline, there is one principle which we must all accept: to avoid actions which could harm others.

❧

We must act together, with mutual respect, accepting disagreements in our views with the aim of ultimately surmounting them. We must see ourselves as human beings first, and stop according absolute priority to economics and politics. All of these elements must be included if we wish to evolve an effective and widespread ethical behavior. This is the only way it will be possible to find urgently needed solutions when severe conflicts, environmental problems, epidemics, famines, and economic upheavals begin to appear at one place or another on the planet. These are the conditions which will enable us to muster a rapid and effective coordination of available resources on such a huge scale.

❧

Solving problems on a scale as vast as that of our planet demands seeing them in a global perspective. This approach means that we must find a way to reconcile individual, social, and national interests, and also be able to adapt ourselves to new circumstances.

❧

We should look at the world and its problems each day as if we were seeing them for the first time.

❧

Enthusiasm, goodwill, determination, and courage are indispensable if we are to face the urgency of certain world events.

❧

The solution to war is neither military, political, nor technological. The nuclear arms race will not prevent conflict. Violence only breeds more violence. The real solution is of a spiritual and ethical order.

❧

The power of arms cannot endure forever. When conditions are right, this power is overturned by democracy and the desire for freedom and justice. The human spirit is always the ultimate winner in this kind of struggle.

❧

Ethical realization is based on giving; a disinterested giving, with no expectation in return; a giving which is impartial and of equal goodwill toward all beings.

❧

Working out a global ethics of behavior is indispensable for furthering the happiness of the planet in general.

❧

The view of the earth from space shows how unreal our human-created borders are. Looking at the image of this blue planet gives a feeling of unity. Everything seems right, consistent, and in its proper place. In comparison, human space-time is lived through differences, competition, power, conflict, and enmity. Nevertheless, the earth remains a whole, and we were all born from this wholeness, all dependent on one another. The future and the very survival of humanity will not be realized unless we accept interdependence (which is the basis of Buddhist teaching) as a vital and undeniable principle of life. The current realities of economics, politics, and ecology make this more obvious every day. Clarity and reflection can bring us more wisdom, so as to make this principle real, and not just virtual, in our lives.

❧

A universal ethics of behavior must be based on human reality, never on religious doctrine.

❧

The current adult generation is too caught up in the mechanisms of the modern world, and dependent on them. It would be difficult, both psychically and physically, to change these acquired habits. Building a better world will come about through education of children.

The strategy for this has two aspects:

Short-term: action relating to environmental problems and human rights.

Long-term: developing spiritual wisdom and teachings, and adapting these to contemporary society.

❧

The founding desire of all political and religious systems is to help human beings to be happy. the means for attaining this goal may often seem contradictory. This is why it is useless to cling to forms. Instead, we must stay with the foundations. We must never lose sight of the truth that human beings are more important than any ideology whatsoever.

❧

Planetary destruction by nuclear weapons is the greatest danger which threatens humanity. We all know the reality of this danger. We are responsible for it. It is time to allow ourselves the means to eliminate it.

Bioethics

Abortion is an act of great violence. A fetus is a human being by its very nature. Killing it means killing a human being, as a general rule. However, each circumstance must be evaluated according to its own specific conditions. If there is a serious risk for the mother or the baby, or if this birth would be disastrous for the family, then one may consider putting an end to this new life. But this should only be a solution of last resort, when all other possibilities have been considered fully.

❧

In some exceptional cases, euthanasia may be appropriate. For example, if a person who is in a permanent coma is being kept alive only by artificial means, and this situation poses great financial difficulties for the family, then euthanasia may be considered. However, if you are faced with such a decision, reflect deeply on the consequences for you, for the dying person, and for the medical personnel.

❧

Whether we are dealing with euthanasia or abortion, the choice always involves the taking of a human life. Each case must be evaluated according to its own characteristics. In all cases, you should examine your own motivation with great honesty. The true nature of your decision is determined by the motivation behind it.

❧

Birth control is not a simple or innocuous subject. Each person should give priority to means which do not involve destroying a fertilized ovum.

❧

In general, scientists have failed to anticipate the impact of certain discoveries. Atomic physics shows this, as does genetic manipulation. The same unconsciousness is at work in the field of economics. The race for short-term profits could create planetary catastrophes.

The Environment

———

Buddhists have always had respect for nature. Preserving the environment is a central concern for them. For a Buddhist, every insect or plant occupies an essential and indispensable place in existence. Even the tiniest micro-organism has a specific role to play in maintaining our ecosystem. Also, Buddhist teachings recognize all living beings as sentient. Every living being has the ultimate potential to realize its Buddha-nature in the course of the many rebirths which constitute its becoming.

❧

All religious and spiritual traditions should engage themselves and their members in protecting the environment.

❧

It is good to be concerned about ecology and animal rights. Such interests help to develop selflessness, generosity, an open heart, and non-violent action.

❧

We commit extremely violent acts toward animals. Consider the way chickens are crowded together inside huge factory-cages under abominable conditions. We abolish their liberty and slaughter them, solely in order to eat them more cheaply. Why do human beings behave in this way? It is partly due to overpopulation. Excessive numbers and aggression often go together, and such actions have hidden repercussions on our inner peace.

❧

Our generation should feel more responsibility and concern about problems of the environment, pollution, and over-population. We should also spare no effort to stop the reckless depletion of our natural resources. If we fail to deal with these things, it may be too late for future generations to find solutions to the catastrophes which we have created.

The Media

It is essential to be well-informed. On the other hand, watching television programs which emphasize sex and violence is harmful to education and to social life. Such programs influence the behavior of children, adolescents, and adults. Sex and violence then serve as a kind of orientation in people's lives. The danger is in the spiritual and human void in which they live. Cut off from wisdom and knowledge, they come to believe that life must be based on this type of behavior. Here, the role of adults and teachers is vital. It is difficult to forbid children to watch TV or see movies. However, it is possible to discuss these media images with those close to us, so as to decipher them. This can help them and us to realize that they are no more than a reflection of a fragmentary human and social reality. What they express is the suffering of people for whom life has been deprived of meaning. Hence it is important to have compassion for them.

❧

The power of the media is considerable. This power should be used for the common good, helping people to become more compassionate and cooperative.

❧

The time people spend watching television is constantly increasing. They have become dependent upon it, and its impact and influence are enormous. Television influences people in their daily lives, in what they think, do, and are.

§

Television producers and directors bear a heavy responsibility. They are major actors in the creation of the modern mentality. They play an important role in the education of children. Adolescent behavior often reflects the violent scenarios which are the main attraction of certain programs. Some youth even find models of behavior there which lead them to commit acts of violence, including murder. The responsibility of these decision-makers is as great as that of political and religious leaders.

§

The power of the media is all the more insidious for being hidden, and often addressed to the unconscious mind.

§

Most human beings live only a virtual life when they identify with television actors, images, and scenes. They are allowing their true life to be stolen.

§

If our everyday life is mostly lived through images on the screen, then our life is controlled by these images, instead of by the reality we experience.

§

An excess of images deposes being in favor of appearance,

which then becomes impervious to all possible expression of being.

❧

The news is always dominated by violence. It sells. However, it is not true that human nature is primarily aggressive and violent. It is also kind and compassionate, and capable of love. It would be only fair for the media to reflect a more balanced and harmonious view of the world and of social life.

The Economy

Poverty, misery, insecurity, and unemployment create untold suffering for some people. Riches, the accumulation of wealth, and anxiety about losing it, create just as great suffering for still others. We need a more just economic system. Everyone's suffering would be lessened. Sharing is a real source of happiness, one which can transform lives.

❧

Some changes are subtle, but transformative. People in science, business, and politics are becoming more interested in spirituality. The material world is revealing its limits, and some leaders are becoming aware of it. This is why they are beginning to look for solutions in realms which only recently seemed irrational to them, and lacking in concrete meaning.

❧

The field of economics will begin to manifest compassion and selflessness when economists become aware of the negative consequences of what they do.

❧

Humanizing finance and economics presupposes more open-mindedness in facing up to the real consequences of current policies in the poorest countries. This awareness is all the more necessary because of the ever-growing social unrest in the richer countries themselves. Some people are now speaking of this unrest as reflecting a "fourth world." A more human financial and economic system is urgently needed now, because it also involves the future of humanity.

❧

Money is obviously necessary, but we make a serious error when we see it as an independent force, especially one which in itself can solve our material and existential problems.

❧

It is more important to have a healthy mind, one which is positive, selfless, and generous, than to accumulate possessions and money.

❧

The North/South imbalance is appalling. Many problems will arise from the injustice of this economic chasm. It would be wiser for people to engage in local action to help each other, so as to prevent the suffering of mass migrations to richer countries, and the growth of religious and political extremism which often results from it. Uprooting oneself is never a happy event.

❧

Possessing much money and using it to help your neighbors is a positive motivation for acquiring it. On the other hand, the obsession with increasing your own profits to the detriment of others can only bring you dreadful suffering, sooner or later. It is this obsession which leads to practices such as mistreating animals, exploiting children, selling arms, and generally treating human beings as if they were slaves.

❧

Wealth can be a form of slavery in itself.

Politics

Politicians and media journalists should have to explain to current generations the catastrophic present and future consequences of their actions.

❧

We all bear responsibility for what happens to society, and for the politicians who represent us. We have a duty to act, making use of the means available to us.

❦

All totalitarian systems come to an end sooner or later. In the history of a country, democratic forces sooner or later have their day.

❦

Investing money in armaments only perpetuates a system based on war. We must work toward a general, massive disarmament. Governments are unwilling to take this step. Yet every non-violent act of resistance which refuses recourse to arms does its part to help the cause of peace and the evolution of conscience.

❦

World peace can only be founded on complete mutual trust. It is incompatible with the maintenance of armament stockpiles which can be used at any moment. It can only be brought about progressively. This hope is not some utopian notion. We must spare no effort to realize it, for the survival of humanity depends on it. This path means we must first acquire skills for the development of our own inner peace, for it is inseparable from outer peace. Then it will become more clear that we can meet the challenge of world peace.

❦

We are all responsible for the attainment of peace at the international level.

❧

Democracy is more just especially because it advocates the separation of legislative and judiciary powers. These must be independent in a well-functioning system.

❧

All politicians need a spiritual life. If they are deprived of this foundation, and merely serve their own interests, they will harm many people.

❧

In is imperative that we establish a group of persons, a kind of "world council of sages," who are humanistically oriented, free of prejudice and special interests, and who give top priority to human welfare. Current governmental representatives strive only on behalf of their own countries, caring little for the needs of others. This is why it is necessary to set up a council of unselfish and responsible people who will make it their task to protect all peoples.

❧

Non-violence is a way of action which is gaining more and more recognition in the world. It now symbolizes a form of strength to most people, whereas formerly it seemed to indicate weakness.

❧

Political, financial, educational, and religious systems are becoming more and more divested of human control.

§

One of the gravest dangers for the world is overpopulation. Yet most politicians are indifferent to this threat to human survival.

§

The Buddhist principle of interdependence necessarily implies that we respect not only human rights, but the rights of children and animals as well, especially if we really want things to change. Political thinking must never neglect any of these areas.

Science

The Dalai Lama has engaged in a growing dialogue with scientists in recent years. The discoveries of quantum physics, as well as advances in neuroscience and astrophysics, seem to be gradually closing the gap which had seemed to separate these different disciplines from Buddhist philosophy and spirituality. Barriers are falling, and new perspectives are being revealed. Human beingness is at the center of these discussions. The dogmas of older science are being upset by the knowledge and experience of great spiritual practitioners and sages.

The spiritual and temporal leader of Tibet maintains a keen interest in anything which could help Buddhism itself to evolve further along the way of knowledge and wisdom. It has always shared with science the same ideal of readiness to abandon any doctrine or teachings which are shown to be in error.

These meetings are characterized by the openness, curiosity, and congeniality of the participants, making these "informal" days of conversation unique and memorable occasions. It is now clear that our problems can never be resolved only by science, technology, and material progress. Peace of mind requires discovering and learning another kind of inner science. The meeting of these two types of science—utterly divergent in appearance, but complementary in truth—gives an extraordinary richness and density to these dialogues.

The cycle from which the following material is taken began in 1987. Two persons were responsible for beginning it: Adam Engle, an American businessman, and Francisco Varela, an internationally renowned figure in systems theory and neuroscience. Ever since that first conversation, scientists from all over the world have come to Dharamsala about every two years to attend these meetings. "The exchanges are intense, effective, and on such a high level that everyone there is transformed," as Varela himself says. He adds that "His Holiness has never found himself lost in these discussions of Western science. His keen intellect penetrates with surprising precision into scientific arguments or accounts of experiments."

Beyond all these favorable signs, it is important to note that these collaborations have avoided being sidetracked into mere sterile intellectual discussion. They often shed light on the leading edges of current scientific experimentation. Here as elsewhere, the primary motivation of the Dalai Lama remains one of service to others.

❧

Even awakened beings do not necessarily understand all the subtleties of modern technology.

❧

Medical traditions which take the whole human being into account seem more effective to me. Mind, body, and environment are linked together. To treat systems while ignoring the others may enable us to treat pathological symptoms, but not the real causes.

❧

Scientific knowledge about matter is considerable. But in regards to the mind, it has access only to the most simple and obvious kinds of manifestations. Such knowledge stops at the very place where Buddhist intellectual, spiritual, philosophical, and empirical knowledge begins.

❧

Nothing has any ultimate beginning or end, neither matter nor spirit. And no one has ever proved the contrary.

❧

The Buddhist tradition would say that a number of Big Bangs preceded the one in which our universe began. Each Big Bang gave birth to a specific world, which evolved, was transformed, and then annihilated in a black hole. A period of absence of any particle succeeded this destruction, and then a new Big Bang occurred, and so on. These cycles of creation/destruction of universes have been going on for an immeasurable time. Time is without origin, beginning, or end.

❦

Human life begins at birth. The physical body begins to form at conception. The spirit then incarnates in the fetus which is forming. Both mind and body are determined by a continuity which precedes all this. This continuity is unique to each being, inherent in their nature. The mother's ovum and the father's sperm participate in creating the body. However, if we go far enough back in the infinite time preceding this, we reach the limits of the visible universe. The Big Bang. Hence the ultimate causes which gave rise to this body are without any fixed or determined beginning. The same is true of spirit.

❦

It is often difficult, especially for Westerners, to understand and accept the Buddhist teaching that neither life nor being has any demonstrable, fixed origin. Granted, this doctrine is difficult to prove. But for Buddhists, to postulate a determinate origin entails more difficulties, because it generates an endless number of contradictions.

❦

Of course science and technology are important. They help us to live better and more comfortably, and give us knowledge which helps to treat pathological conditions more effectively. They also help us to expand our knowledge of ourselves, the world, and the universe. However, the truth still remains that human beings give far too much importance to material realities. Spirituality is just as essential to life. The balanced way is to know how to reconcile these two aspects, so as to prevent the growth of dehumanizing influences.

❧

Science and technology do not help human beings to face and understand their existential problems.

7

RELIGION

In the beginning, human beings had common rituals. Before humanity began to spread and differentiate all over the planet, people had a common symbolic system inspired by a perception of greater dimensions of being.

The variety of animistic traditions show that, although there is a universal reverence and attention given to unknown and invisible forces, determining the very rhythms of daily life, there is still a great difference in spiritual practices among people of different races and ethnicities. Each tradition had its own independent existence, its own real powers and invocations for healing, peace, and war. The saga of good and evil depended on human beings and their relations with their natural surroundings.

As civilizations developed and grew powerful, people forgot how to listen to the etheric language of the trees, the rain, the sun, and wandering spirits. The chants of the American Indians were silenced, and the doors which connected us to parallel universes were shut. Good, Evil, innocence, and guilt became the reality and responsibility of humans themselves.

This responsibility has sometimes helped us to overcome old fears and limits, as well as to discover new frontiers, self-knowledge, and communion with one another. The other realms, whose perception we lost in the process, then became accessible primarily through the symbolism of the heavens and hells described in almost all traditions, including Buddhism. Mostly, the emphasis moved from inner to outer, through worship of an almighty Creator, often entailing fear and submission.

But mystics have always given priority to inner realization, where the union with transcendent Reality is total, absolute, luminous, and irreversible.

In this transfiguration, the "Kingdom of God" is here and now, in this world, which is also their inner world.

Mystics live this same Union in all traditions, whether they are called Hindu, Christian, Muslim, Jewish, Buddhist.... When we let go of categories and distinctions, the apparent diversity fades into the background, and human beingness becomes unique and universal once again.

Buddhism

The purpose of a spiritual path is to guide those who desire to discover their fundamental nature, and to help them live the inner Unity which flows from this quest.

This Unity also offers peace and happiness. In everyday life, our thoughts and actions are often in disharmony, expressing our contradictions and fears. Duality is characteristic of the world of illusions. Unity opens us into total knowledge of ourselves and others.

❧

An authentic spiritual path endeavors to reconcile disciples with themselves, and consequently with others. This is a process which requires both inner and outer skills. The inner and outer worlds are interdependent, and mirror each other. The disciple's progress on the path is reflected in the realization of inner practices through actions and words.

❧

If you follow a spiritual path, it is foolish and vain to flatter or deceive yourself about your inner evolution. An authentic path is always a road with dangers, including precipitous drops off the side. Any false step can make you fall, and reality will catch up with you. Do not commit yourself lightly.

❧

The Way is very demanding. It requires humility, simplicity, sincerity, and letting go of our attachments. It involves many trying experiences, which test our courage and determination.

❧

You can fool yourself into believing you are generous, selfless, and sincere. You can convince yourself and others that you have special talents and powers. But these talents and powers are of no use. They will not make you into a better human being. You are still caught in the world of appearances and illusion. Only your deeds and exemplary way of living symbolize and validate your commitment to the Way.

❧

Life is like a catalyst. It obliges us to confront ourselves as we really are. If our will to self-transformation is impeccable, then every situation, whether happy or unhappy, becomes a practice in itself, and an instrument for inner evolution.

❧

Why postpone the moment of confrontation with that which animates you and characterizes you? The day when you accept this confrontation will be the day when peace is born within you. Your fears will diminish and happiness will gradually begin to construct your existences.

❧

The Buddhist tradition is a kind of science of the mind and spirit. It is a complex tradition, which includes religious, metaphysical, philosophical, and humanistic aspects. The religious aspects includes rituals, initiations, and meditation practices. These are based on faith, analysis, an understanding of certain concepts, and on experience. Practice and theory are complementary in forming the whole.

❧

Spirituality is based on a training and discipline whose goal is mastery of the mind.

❧

To engage oneself in a spiritual practice without learning how to master one's emotions of craving, aggression, violence, and hatred, leads to far greater suffering than before, both in one-self and in others.

❧

Being ordained as a monk or a nun is not enough to confer this status. The monk's robe does not reflect his inner evolution. Religious life has duties and obligations, especially those involving service to others. Self-transformation is based on daily practice and study of the teachings. To wear the robes of a renunciate while remaining attached to the world of appearances and illusions debases the role that is symbolized. Stay with the examples of the Buddha and other great masters of the past. The trials they went through will guide you and help you on this path.

❧

Authentic masters are living models and examples. Their acts bear witness to the depth of their practice.

❧

All commerce in religious objects is a negative act when it is motivated by profit. On the other hand, the restoration of ancient teachings, texts, and damaged ritual objects, or pictorial representations of the life of Gautama Buddha and other great masters is a beneficial activity which aids the transmission of Buddhism.

❧

Faith should not be based on ignorance, but on analysis and reflection.

❧

In Tibetan Buddhism, people often have questions about the "blessing" given by masters to disciples. During these blessings, the specific qualities of the master, and all the grace and spiritual realization which he received from his own masters, are transmitted to those present. These blessings are thus passed uninterruptedly from teacher to teacher, through centuries of lineages, from the origin, ever since the Buddha himself. During these special moments, the master becomes like a transparent channel. It is a great privilege for a disciple to have the chance to receive this subtle and intangible gift.

❧

It is extremely beneficial to receive blessings, but they alone cannot transform you. A blessing is like a seed planted in your inner being. If you do not water it and nourish it with your discipline and your determination, this plant will wilt.

❧

Buddhist monks take a vow of poverty so as to reduce their attachment to material things. Donations to monks or nuns are used for the community as a whole, both religious and secular, according to the need.

❧

For Buddhist monks, the last meal of the day is traditionally the one at high noon. Mastering the needs of the body diminishes attachment to it.

❧

My role is to make my knowledge available to others, without proselytizing. The essential thing is not to convince someone of the validity of Buddhist teachings, but but of the urgency of developing our human potential. This is the only way we can ever transform the world.

❧

For me, it is unthinkable to convert someone to my religion. This is not true respect for others. On the other hand, if someone comes to me who wants to follow this way, then it is my duty to respond to their questions.

❧

Compassion engenders non-violence. This attitude is a guideline for all practitioners. Buddhist philosophy is based on the principle of the interdependence of all things, beings, and phenomena. Non-violence, compassion, and awareness of interdependence should guide all our actions.

❧

Some Westerners express curiosity about Buddhism. People are always interested in following new trends, whether in spiritual or in other domains—this is basic to human nature. Buddhism is defined as a science of the spirit, and the word "science" appeals to Westerners. Also, the analysis of the mental and emotional phenomena of Buddhist practices makes good use of their intellectual capacities. Also, the Buddhist insistence on unifying knowledge and wisdom cannot fail to affect them, because this union brings peace and equanimity.

❦

A tradition which surrenders to fanaticism, sacrificing reflection and pragmatism, is a tradition doomed to disappear.

❦

Buddhist philosophy is based on four fundamental concepts:
—All things are impermanent.
—Neither visible nor invisible phenomena have any existence in themselves. They are interdependent parts of the whole, the results of a chain of causes and conditions.
—Negativity (i.e., the source of suffering) can and must be transformed.
—The goal is awakening, inner peace, realization of Nirvana.

❦

Understanding the principle of rebirth leads to equanimity: in other words, a kind of equality of being and behaving in relation to all beings. Buddhist tradition says that at one time or another during the vast, numberless cycles of existence we have been through, all beings have been our parents, our children, or our friends. If so, why judge one as superior to another? We act in this way only out of ignorance.

❦

The Eastern concept of karma is closest to the Western concept of destiny. But the rules which determine these two do not follow the same principles. Karma means action. This action takes place when causes and conditions have ripened, and come together in a given moment. It is a complex process, and we are responsible. This means that our words, deeds, and behavior leave imprints on our consciousness from one life to another.

❧

Intellectual knowledge is inseparable from the intelligence of the heart for those who practice the Buddhist way. Each nourishes and completes the other. A life dominated by knowledge without openness of the heart cannot express generosity and selflessness. Such knowledge is dry and sterile. It is merely one of the manifestations of ego.

❧

The goal of all religions is to alleviate the sufferings of the world. Human nature is similar in all continents of the globe. The mental discipline and knowledge of one's emotions taught by Buddhism can serve as a skillful means of realizing happiness, whatever one's culture, tradition, or religion.

❧

True Buddhism is not a dogma. It is based on knowledge, wisdom, and experience.

❧

Buddhist teaching must adapt itself to the capacities of each human being. The same principles are thus transmitted in different ways, appropriate to different listeners.

❧

Taking refuge is an important Buddhist ritual, similar to that of baptism in the Catholic church. This means that becoming a Buddhist is not a thing to be undertaken lightly. This decision affects not only this life, but also many future existences.

❧

Never abandon your roots and native tradition without long and deep reflection. Such a decision has real consequences. It is entirely possible to make good use of certain Buddhist teachings and practices, so as to develop non-violence, tolerance, compassion, and generosity, without becoming a convert to this religion.

❧

Cultivating peace of mind is at the heart of Buddhist practice. It is this inner peace, or lack of it, that determines how we behave toward others. It shapes our way of seeing the world, and influences everything in our life.

❧

If science ever detects errors in our teachings, then we must not hesitate to reconsider them. Rigid attachment to scripture is a mistake.

❧

The Buddhist tradition is not uniform. It includes a large number of different schools, yet all of them take the words of the Buddha as their foundation. The Buddha is a historical figure whose existence is solidly established, and also a human being who demonstrated that we are all capable of realizing the perfection of our being.

Other Religions

The Gospels say that the sun shines upon all of us equally. This is a symbol of true compassion, and expresses the truth that it is offered to all beings alike, whether friends or enemies.

❧

The Bible says that God made human beings in his own image. If you make good use of this scripture, it can help you to develop equanimity. If you accept that we are all creatures made in the image of God, then it would be contradictory for you to harbor judgments, preferential emotions, and fears regarding your fellow creatures.

❧

In all religious traditions, the individual mind should remain free to choose. Its learning process should be progressive, and in keeping with its level of maturity. A will which has been broken and bridled, a consciousness which is hypnotized by imposed concepts, can produce a rebellious and troubled mind. In the long run, such conditioning makes it more difficult to deal with the trials of life.

❧

It is not necessary to follow a religion in order to be a charitable, compassionate, and generous human being.

❧

I respect all religions, because they have the same aim: to enable human beings to develop what is best in them. They all point to the path of inner peace. Their doctrinal differences are aspects of the cultures and civilizations in which they were formed.

❧

It is not advisable to solicit someone who is not a Buddhist to recite mantras, receive blessings or initiations, or even to take medicines which have been sanctified by certain rituals. These practices only make sense for those who have taken the Buddhist path. To disregard this is like asking a Buddhist, Jew, or Moslem to take Christian communion. It is not necessary to participate in Christian rites in order to respect Jesus Christ and his teaching.

❧

The important thing is not to convert to some religion. The important thing is to transform yourself so as to contribute to the peace of the world.

❧

Human diversity justifies the large number of religions that exist. Just as our needs differ regarding food and clothing, so do our spiritual needs. Buddhism does not require belief in a Creator-God as a fundamental postulate. This concept can be a help for some people, but an obstacle for others. It is not essential what we believe, or do not believe, regarding a determinate origin of all things. The essential thing is what we do with our beliefs, how we apply them, and live them.

✿

Establishing a dialogue that includes all religions will help us to understand each other and work together for the good of humanity.

✿

An overall consensus of all religions can only be based upon their common wish to contribute to the welfare of all beings, and upon their shared determination to do everything possible to establish peace in the world. This is both a humanitarian and a spiritual consensus. In order for it to be effective, each party concerned must act both cooperatively and on their own.

✿

The metaphysical, philosophical, and theological polemics stirred up by certain individuals are only intellectual theories which are completely irrelevant to our happiness. If your desire is for the happiness of others, then forget these polemics and divisive discussions.

✿

All those remarkable people who mobilize their contemporaries toward good acts, drawing widespread praise and admiration, have certain common characteristics: kindness, compassion, generosity, selflessness, courage, and a steadfast caring for others. Often these individuals may be great practitioners in some religious tradition or other, but their real interest is in how they act and behave in general. Even if their beliefs are a great source of support for them, it is for the quality of their actions that most people value them, not for their beliefs.

❧

It is only over the long term, and through the way of life that they embody, that human beings reveal the true depth of the spiritual dimension they inhabit.

❧

Whether Christian, Moslem, Jew, or unbeliever, anyone can make use of Buddhist meditation techniques so as to discover happiness and inner peace.

❧

To harbor the idea that everyone should be Buddhist engenders extremist and fanatical behavior.

❧

One single religion for all humanity would not serve the happiness of individuals, because it would not be adapted to their diversity.

❧

If you choose to follow a religion, practice it sincerely and with all your force. Cultural and religious mishmash creates confusion in people's minds.

❧

Knowledge of a religion is only real if it is based on inner experience which leads to living its principles in every moment of ordinary life.

❧

Every religion advocates ethical principles which guide its members in their behavior, so as to develop human qualities such as generosity, tolerance, and selflessness.

❧

Interfaith dialogue leads to knowledge and respect for others. Through this process, strong links can be established between people whose beliefs are apparently very different from each other.

❧

No religion should ever be a source of discord, conflict, or (worst of all) war—neither among its own adherents, nor with those of different faiths.

❧

The majority of people alive on this planet today are not religious. However, our duty as religious people is to help them become more tolerant and generous, not to proselytize. Education is our main resource for this, and it involves adults, not just youth. Society in general also has a major role and responsibility in this.

❧

In Buddhism the law of causality is said to work through numerous cycles of existence. In many other religions, the notion of reincarnation is not considered to be meaningful. Yet the fact still remains, beyond these differing points of view, that all these religions are very concerned with the principle of causality. And they all conclude that misery engenders misery, and goodness engenders goodness.

❧

The concept of a Creator-God is difficult for a Buddhist to admit. Although theistic and non-theistic religions will continue to differ on this point, it in no way prevents dialogue between them.

❧

The lives of Jesus and Buddha, founders of two of the greatest world religions, have many points in common. And the main one is that they both lived fully what they taught.

❧

For all who follow a spiritual path with the aim of freeing themselves from the illusions of this world, there will be trials. And these require will, commitment, and a desire to evolve.

❧

Do not believe that prayers are useless because you cannot see their effects, which are not always expressed in tangible physical results. The effects of prayer are often subtle, acting especially on the person who prays and radiating through them to the rest of the universe and to all beings.

🌿

Never confuse religious life with spiritual life.

🌿

No religious revelation or culture is necessary in order to develop compassion, open-mindedness, and generosity. However, following a spiritual path may help to understand the larger role that these qualities play in the fulfillment of human life.

🌿

Human beings are always blaming God, destiny, karma, or whatever for all sorts of evils. Yet we have a certain freedom of choice, and our responsibility is to use it well, and to not lose courage. We must not give in to cowardice, especially in situations which we ourselves have brought about.

🌿

If you believe in God, do not expect him to do everything for you. Do your part also in taking charge of your life.

🌿

Some see God as an omnipotent father. Others see him in a more mystical way, not as a divine being with more or less human attributes, but as a transcendence which forms the very foundation of being.

❧

A Tibetan proverb says that an especially clever person can join seemingly contradictory arguments so plausibly that listeners will be convinced that both are true. Dialogue between religions is one thing, but wanting to establish agreement between them at any price is an entirely different thing. Trying to set up a universal religion which satisfies everyone is futile and dangerous for human beings. We are different from each other, and we should choose the religion that is most appropriate for us. This is how inner transformation can happen. Each tradition contains and teaches specific practices which have been worked out over centuries. Random experimentation has no place in such a system. Each way has its own rigorous and precise learning process.

❧

Ethical and spiritual practice are fundamental areas of convergence between Christianity and Buddhism.

❧

The principle of interdependence of all beings and phenomena, a fundamental concept of Buddhist philosophy, excludes the possibility of a Creator-God as an existent being. From the Buddhist point of view, the existence of any being is the result of a chain of causes and conditions. This is in keeping with a metaphysics in which the origin of the universe is eternal and determinate.

❦

Tara as goddess of compassion, and Mary as symbol of universal love, play the same role in our two traditions.

❦

Every Buddhist should see Jesus as a being of great spiritual realization, who placed his life in service to others.

❦

The notion of the demonic occurs frequently in the Christian gospels. It seems to me that there is no validity to the notion of deadly demonic forces which come from beyond to dominate us and bring about our downfall. When the Christian scriptures speak of these entities, they are probably referring to the negative emotions which exist in all of us.

❦

When Jesus says that he has not come to judge or condemn, is he not also implying that we are responsible for our actions? And that it is these actions which will "judge" us, not some all-powerful being external to ourselves?

❦

Commitment to a spiritual path is absolutely not something which will magically resolve all our problems, nor those of society. But in the long run it is undeniable that such a path provides skillful means for uprooting the negative tendencies which control us.

❧

Christians believe that God created us all in his own image. Buddhists believe that we all possess the Buddha-nature. The terms of these beliefs differ, but they share a common idea.

❧

The Christian tradition also affirms the same divine nature within all beings. If this is so, why treat some as friends and others as enemies?

❧

The Gospels insist on one point which is also at the heart of our Buddhist practices: the equality of all beings.

❧

A person's spiritual progress is not a function of what tradition they belong to. Their evolution depends on their own capacities.

❧

In this world, there is no universal truth. One truth may have many different facets. Its meaning will depend upon how it is decoded through our intellectual, philosophical, cultural, and religious prisms.

❧

Anyone who suffers and expresses their suffering through violent acts or words is still a rare and precious being. We should consider them as a treasure.

The same thing applies to those who behave selfishly, as in the parable of the prodigal son told by Jesus in the Gospels. Such people show us how to go beyond ourselves, how to forgive. They are teachers on our path.

❧

The Gospel passages which relate the transfiguration of Jesus after his entry into the tomb express a theme which recurs in all major religions. The experiences undergone by great mystics can indeed lead to physical transformations. Tibetans use metaphors to speak of such phenomena, so as to render them accessible to the popular imagination. It is important to speak about this process—not because of the spiritual powers it involves, but so as to inspire even greater devotion in disciples. This devotion will render their practice many times more powerful.

❧

Great practitioners must share their progress with others on the way, without any trace of pride or ostentation. It is through their example that others are shown the means to the same realization. Love and compassion guide the great practitioners in this giving of themselves.

❧

The metaphor of light recurs in all religions. For a Buddhist, light is a symbol of wisdom and knowledge. It vanquishes darkness, the symbol of our ignorance.

❧

If you believe that your concept of God is the only one which contains truth and knowledge, then you deny other traditions. Dialogue then becomes impossible. To impose one's own belief on others, to proselytize, can only provoke reactions of rejection from those to whose faith and belief you deny authenticity.

❧

The fact of being born a Buddhist, Christian, Moslem, or Jew does not make you an authentic practitioner of your tradition. It is what you do with your life, in relation to the teachings you receive, that testifies to the validity of your religious conviction.

❧

The great religious ethical principles are born out of a perception of the range of negative actions of which humanity is capable. All these systems condemn things such as theft, rape, and murder. These laws are based upon the exigency of respect for all living beings and for nature. They take into account our individual and collective needs, as well as those of animals.

❧

Every political or religious ideology contains the seeds of limitation and fanatical excess. First and foremost, we are human beings. It is better to dwell upon the qualities we share as such, than upon writings which may be badly understood and interpreted.

❧

The survival of the Jewish tradition is based upon faith and upon the transmission of its practices. In spite of the unimaginable horrors of the Holocaust, and of many generations of persecution and suffering, this tradition has remained intact and alive. This is because it includes a true philosophical wisdom which has been lived in the hearts of many people. This manifests a great strength and impressive determination.

❧

Certain forms of Jewish meditation on compassion and selflessness are very close to Buddhist meditations. To visualize the suffering being experienced by people we know, or by those who are victims of natural catastrophes or famines, helps to put our own suffering in perspective. Both Buddhist and Jewish tradition make great efforts to open individuals' hearts and teach them generosity.

❧

Whether or not one follows a certain religion must be a personal choice.

❧

Some religions claim that their ethical principles can only be realized through God's help. This kind of belief can lead to an implicit condemnation of anyone who does not belong to a theistic religion. But spiritual progress does not depend on what religion we belong to. It depends on our will to transform ourselves.

❧

The future of humanity and the future of religion are closely linked. Each must evolve together.

❧

The ways of God are unfathomable, say the Christian scriptures. This belief can be a help and support in certain circumstances. Yet it can also lead to a certain fatalism which is not helpful in daily life.

❧

The belief in a divine creator can lead to imagining that certain trials have been set up by an all-powerful God as tests of our faith, courage, determination, or strength. Some people who think in this way push themselves beyond their limits, always trying to determine what their responsibility is in every difficult situation. Others simply submit to the suffering as if it alone could bring redemption, and live like sacrificial victims.

❧

The future of religions all over the world depends on their capacity to be of service to all.

7

BUDDHIST TEACHINGS
AND PRACTICES

Our dreams are limited and truncated by the reality of existence. This confrontation with disappointment leads us to question the meaning of life and death, of our place in the world, and of the purpose of creation. Then our search begins, and its questions, and answers, will differ according to our personality and also according to the intensity of our thirst for truth. The answers offered by the Buddha, based on his experience, can find an echo in each of us. For this great Sage knew how to teach on different levels, always adapted to his listeners.

Teachings and practices free the ego-bound mind from its chains, offering skillful means for progressing at our own pace and according to our own capacities, so as to preserve the unbelievable potential which is ours to realize within this very human adventure. It is both an individual and a shared adventure, driving us into the heart of ourselves and also inviting us to participate in the voyage of others. It is a true initiation, an extreme and necessary denuding in which we lose our certitudes and our habits. We have to cross this desert—our own desert of ignorance, selfishness, fears, and little deaths, which we are so reluctant to recognize and abandon—and pass through all these griefs before we can meet the light of Wisdom.

———

Teachings and practices reveal the immensity, the availability, diversity, and adaptability of a unique in-between space. This space is vital in order for the true View to emerge out of our torment, doubt, and pettiness. This View must grow to include the world, so that it does not wither at the sight of our most alienated emotions. Anchoring itself in that dimension which had previously been hidden like a rug under our feet, it spreads and unravels the cords of the net which has caught and strangled us, the net which we ourselves have woven. It dissolves and banishes the darkness, giving us a sense of discrimination, authenticity, and truth. It shows us that the shadow already contains the light at its source.

It is this powerful and clairvoyant View, this Light of Wisdom and Knowledge, which informs the thinking and action of the great practitioners, uniting solar and lunar rays in one transcendent radiance. Indeed, it is this same Light which illumines the present moment with a crystalline, joyous, and humble clarity. To live in it is to live with total confidence and openness of being.

The Dharma

The Buddha's life began like that of any human being, preceded by a great number of cycles of births and deaths, entailing suffering, pain, joy, and many emotions. But regardless of the circumstances, his spiritual practice and compassion guided him in his choices and sustained him in his trials. In his last existence, when he was born as Prince Gautama Shakyamuni, he became a Buddha—which means an awakened being, free of all attachment and illusion. He had shown proof of unrelenting will and determination over a tremendous period of time—this is a truth which we all too often forget. Like children, we hope that we might somehow escape this aspect of the path. It is an absurd hope, for if Gautama himself had to go through these things in order to awaken, why should it be otherwise for us?

❧

Buddhist education is only partly theoretical. Intellectual knowledge must live and mature in our inner being, in our heart. It must be understood, experienced, refined, and explored in every instant of daily life.

❧

The Buddha is often described as a great therapist. His teachings are like prescriptions, designed to help beings free themselves from suffering. His different treatments are adapted to us as individuals, according to our needs and capacities.

❧

Practice works upon us so as to stabilize and regulate our emotional states.

❧

When you are overwhelmed by suffering, think of others whose inner torments and physical tortures are worse than yours.

Yet do not indulge in any morbid or masochistic thoughts. Such reflection should instead awaken your capacity to give. Offer up the pain you are going through to all these other beings who suffer: dedicate the terrible emotions you are feeling to them. This simple act of dedication, this symbolic gift of yourself, even though you are caught up in self-centeredness, will enable you to gradually conquer your egoism. And this offering will also act on subtle levels, so as to help both you and those to whom you make the dedication to overcome trials.

❧

Motivation and determination empower each other, and give us victory over all obstacles to building our confidence and inner strength.

❧

Wisdom and compassion are the foundations of the Buddhist way.

❧

The consciousness which is the foundation of mind is not quantifiable. It is pure and total knowledge, beyond all concepts.

❧

We are responsible for the causes of our suffering. We have knowledge of certain mechanisms which we set up, and which determine these causes. If we really desire to put an end to these hellish cycles, we can do it. It suffices to decide to set aside time to work on this.

❧

Some people like to be in my presence. Yet I am really just an ordinary human being. My only qualities are that I never wish harm toward others, and that I make every effort to increase my ability to give. I will do everything I can to help others to develop their own generosity.

❧

Before placing our trust in someone, we examine their behavior and their words. We should do no less when it comes to the Buddha's words. Are his teachings reliable? Have they really proven their value over the centuries? And the people we meet who currently embody his teachings—are they different from most of the people we know? How so? Only direct experience of these teachings can give us the answers we seek.

❧

Buddhist practice can be summed up in two principles:
— Do not harm others. This will bring you great satisfaction.
— Know the principle of interdependence, and experience it in your life, in beings, in phenomena, and in consciousness. This practical, inner knowledge brings happiness.

❧

Discipline of the mind can only be learned through a progressive and organized process. Our faults must never be hidden or denied. Instead, they are transmuted in the course of a long alchemical process. Their negative energy is transformed into positive energy. This is the same mechanism which rules light and darkness. The germ of light is already present in darkness. When conditions are right, the darkness will gradually give birth to radiant light. If the psychic space now occupied by our complexes is reduced, the resulting empty space can be inhabited by the corresponding positive qualities and emotions.

❧

In spiritual practice, our teacher and guide is also our mirror. They reflect our evolution without judging us. Their encouragements sustain us, yet we must be mindful, so that these do not also reinforce our pride. Certain of our teacher's remarks may also hurt us, but they are indispensible, for they show us where we need to place our efforts. During some periods we will need both compliments and critiques in order to make progress. This will continue until the day when we become able to hear our true inner master. Yet this does not signal the end of our relationship with the teacher who has accompanied us for so many years in this world of cycles. We continue to have a relationship with the teacher, but now it is a different one.

❧

A Buddhist teacher should only speak of what they themselves know through direct experience. If what they are teaching is only theoretical, your time would be better spent in reading books.

❧

Everything is illusion. Changing emotions, happy times, un-happy times, all of them are illusory. Understanding of the real nature of phenomena frees us from appearances.

❧

Uninformed people like to engage in vain discussions about what is known as the "third eye" in Tibetan tradition. Is it real? Or symbolic? Such discussions are futile. It would be better to have eyes spread all over one's body, like Tara, god-dess of compassion, so as to be able to see all the sufferings of the world and help to alleviate them.

❧

If we do not practice, then having a special relation with a spiritual master is of no help on the way.

❧

Helping others implies that we have already passed through different phases of our spiritual path. Our effectiveness will depend on what we have lived and understood. One must have known suffering oneself in order to find words and ges-tures which can alleviate others' suffering. We must have been through the trial of doubt ourselves before we can help an-other face such a trial.

The Law of Cause and Effect

It is possible to create and accumulate a large amount of very good karma in one lifetime. Karma is based on causes and effects. If you devote all your efforts toward making yourself into a good and generous being, the results which flow from this will necessarily be positive.

🕊

In the law of causality, the motivation behind an action is more important than the action itself. It is our intention which is the source of our responsibility.

🕊

Every situation, whether individual or planetary, results from a chain of causes and conditions generated by human beings through numerous existences.

🕊

Our shared perception of the world gives rise to a collective karma.

🕊

The Buddhist law of causality applies to all beings and all phenomena. This cannot include a determinate, primordial origin which is created by a God external to the process.

❧

The universe, our existence, our consciousness, and all events only exist in relation to each other, comprising an incalculable number of causes and conditions. However far back we go through endless time and space, we will always see this principle at work.

❧

We always have a certain freedom of choice. Spiritual practice counteracts some of the negative karma we have created over lifetimes. Waiting passively for painful events to be over with does not help to overcome them, nor to lessen their impact.

❧

The process of the law of causality is complex. Do not judge a person, thinking that you fully understand this law. Never condemn them in your thoughts because they seem to have a "bad karma" which is bringing them great suffering. Most of the great masters have suffered terrible and painful trials before becoming realized beings.

❧

Understanding of the law of causality transforms our view of our own life and that of others. It changes our way of thinking and acting, and opens our mind and its world to a perspective of infinite dimensions.

❧

The true nature of an action cannot be judged according to moral principles. An act is positive if it generates happiness, and negative if it is a source of suffering.

Consciousness, the Self, and Phenomena

Nothing exists in and of itself. Nothing can ever manifest in a separate and independent manner. Life is like a dream. None of the objects and persons that figure in it have any autonomous or permanent reality.

❧

The phenomenon of reincarnation is characterized by a continuum of consciousness—our spirit, or mind—transmitted from lifetime to lifetime. This continuum undergoes constant transformation, appearing as a particular quality of consciousness from one instant to another. This continuum is not the same as what scientists call "consciousness"—in other words, ordinary consciousness which changes according to physical and mental perceptions and sensations from the phenomenal world.

❧

"Everything is impermanent." This is the law which rules all cycles of existence.

❧

To be attached to beings and objects is like trying to hug a rainbow. Understanding of the true nature of phenomena frees us of the desire to possess them.

❧

The "ego" must be distinguished from the "self" which desires to experience the Buddha's realization through compassion and love for others. The courage, determination, and self-confidence of the latter is founded upon a sense of identity which is not some solid, permanent entity separate from others. This sense of "I" is free of selfishness and egoism.

❧

All beings and phenomena exist in complete interdependence. This is why no entity can be permanent, solid, independent, and real in itself.

❧

Contrary to appearances, beings and phenomena have no intrinsic existence. They are like images reflected in a mirror, illusory and unreal in themselves. They are only meaningful in a conventional, nominal, conceptual sense.

❧

In Buddhism, when we speak of the middle way, of interdependence, or of emptiness, we are really speaking of a single concept. Emptiness is also dependent on causes and conditions. It cannot be equated with the concept of nothingness, nor with any eternal reality.

❧

As long as we live as separate beings, unconscious of how tightly we are linked with others; as long as we are unable to acknowledge that we are only the outcome of various influences; and as long as we think that we possess a specific identity, it will be impossible for us to understand the truth that all phenomena are void of any intrinsic existence.

❧

Perceptions are deceiving, because they arise from our senses. The manifestation of appearances does not express the true nature of these phenomena.

Nirvana and Awakening

To dissolve illusions means to understand and experience the truth that the ego, phenomena, and emotions have no existence in themselves. This direct perception of emptiness destroys the very roots of the imprints which the mind has accumulated through illusion.

❧

To realize emptiness is to form a correct view of reality. It is not a rejection of the world in which we are evolving, but a different way of seeing it.

❧

Nirvana is often designated as "the other side" of the cycles of lives and deaths that we pass through. It is what lies beyond ignorance. This present cycle of existences is ruled by negative emotions and destructive tendencies. It will continue to be, until we transform them.

❧

Realization of nirvana, the ultimate goal of the Buddhist way, is supreme liberation from the world's sufferings. Its quest is founded upon compassion and selflessness, on the desire to help others, and on the ability to do so when the goal has been attained.

❧

Wisdom, radiance, clarity, grace, and knowledge of emptiness open the mind to infinite dimensions, beyond concepts and beyond time and space. And at the same time, they reconnect the mind with the world, in consciousness.

❧

Like any concept or phenomenon, emptiness has no intrinsic, determinate, autonomous, or permanent reality.

❧

"Emptiness is form. Form is emptiness." This Buddhist proverb expresses the interdependence which underlies all things. This principle applies just as well to emptiness itself.

❧

At a certain point in their practice, disciples must abandon all physical and conceptual attachments. This letting-go is the sign of a limitless opening of the heart and absolute confidence in the way.

Practice

When you encounter a problem, don't remain passive. Look for a solution. If a solution exists, you will find it. Why worry about it? Even if there is no solution, it is useless to be afraid. Fear and worry only add to your distress and torment.

❧

Prayer is a daily reminder of our spiritual commitment.

❧

Prayer and chanting of mantras diminish the impact of the fears which beset us.

❧

Authentic spirituality is practiced in every moment.

❧

The goal of meditation is the discipline, training, and mastery of the mind. This inner development requires a sustained, daily effort.

❧

The Tibetan tradition is characterized by two categories of meditations:
—Analytic meditation, based on repeated analysis and reflection upon an object, a concept, or a situation. This enables the disciple to investigate the intellectual and theoretical assumptions which they are employing. When these data are confirmed, the mind dwells in a clear, luminous, and peaceful space. At this point, meditation becomes contemplation.
—Meditation upon a single point, which trains the mind in concentration.

❧

Meditation upon mental calmness facilitates concentration and helps to understand the illusory nature of phenomena.

❧

Meditation upon impermanence and suffering engenders renunciation of all forms of attachment.

❧

The quality of your meditation is more important than the amount of time you devote to it.

❧

Discipline of the mind involves a progressive sequence spread out over time:
—Learning to develop positive qualities.
—Ripening of the conviction that we are on the right path. This conviction impels us to educate and transform ourselves.
—Manifesting great determination in effort and in action.

❧

The development of self-mastery requires time, involving years of trials and unflagging effort.

❧

The pain, problems, and trials we encounter on a spiritual path are not obstacles. They are in fact the means by which we make progress and acquire a larger perspective. This enables us to evaluate situations with a long term view, instead of one dominated by the immediacy of emotions.

❧

If your goal is clear and well-defined, and if you are lucid and realistic about your ability to achieve it, then your motivation and effort will overcome obstacles which appear along the way.

❧

If you are to advance along the way, then every moment must be informed by mindfulness and examination of the motives behind your thoughts and actions.

❧

If you constantly question the importance of your practice, you weaken yourself inwardly. The goal of spiritual realization starts sliding to second place in your priorities. And then your determination and motivation waver, and begin to fade away. And finally you stop practicing altogether.

❧

Ignorance gives rise to the belief in an autonomous, permanent existence of visible or invisible phenomena. This denies both the law of causality and the principle of interdependence which joins all things, including consciousness, with the rest of the universe. Wisdom and knowledge give rise to the true view, which recognizes the illusory nature of appearances.

❧

Here are some of the main obstacles to practice:
— Laziness. This prevents us from realizing our objectives.
— Inertia.
— Discouragement. This is the sign of a lack of confidence in oneself and in the way.
— Impatience.
— Pride.
— An excessive, deluded craving for nirvana.
— Lack of concentration and mindfulness.
— An insatiable desire for worldly experiences and objects of pleasure.

❧

Certain rules of practice should not be applied stupidly and without reflection. In special situations and in cases of necessity, we must be prepared drop them.

🐦

Spiritual training has been structured and validated by generations of teachers and disciples, and follows a determined, precise order. Each step is important, and none should be eliminated. If you are building a house, you follow a given plan and schedule, building the foundations before the outer parts. Only when the whole thing is finished do you decorate the interior. The same principles apply to the spiritual path.

🐦

Freedom from the cycles of existence requires practice over a number of lifetimes.

🐦

A rebellious mind is the cause of untold suffering.

🐦

Mindfulness is like a leash which restrains the undisciplined mind, and keeps it from dispersing and losing itself. It serves as a constant reminder that the mind's task is to acquire mastery of the emotions, thoughts, words, and actions which it generates.

🐦

Effort is necessary at the beginning of practice. Later, in keeping with your progress on the way, your own interest and need to practice take priority. Then you practice with pleasure, finding great joy in this learning process.

❧

When they reach a certain level of practice, great masters retire from the world for a period. Beyond the reach of distractions, they consecrate their life to the way.

❧

It is certain that you will never transform yourself by putting off your practice until tomorrow,

❧

We are here to serve all beings. In your first steps upon the Way, accepting this idea requires an effort of great humility. On the other hand, when your practice opens your inner understanding to the truth that we are not separate beings, but are all linked through interdependence, your service to others is spontaneous, and its humility natural and infinite. This is because you are animated by universal love and compassion.

❧

The mind is a rebellious thing. It wanders restlessly and seeks diversion whenever we attempt to channel it or train it in concentration. Its worst enemies are excitement and indolence.

❧

The mind prefers to lose itself in the past and the future, concocting plans which immerse it in the world of phenomena, rather than to develop mindfulness and presence in the here and now. The present moment appears boring to the mind, especially when it is not being offered a wild ride by the emotions.

❧

The mind itself can also be an object of our meditation. The mind must learn to let go of attachment to concepts, emotions, memories, and projections. Then it will be able to observe these things pass by in succession, as if watching clouds pass in the sky. Once this ability is achieved, the mind can deal with all cajoling and wheedling by simply recalling its true nature, which is radiance and clarity. Mind concentrating upon mind—this is both the subject and the object of the experiment.

❧

The best protection you can receive is not external. It is not something bestowed by a master, nor emitted by sacred relics. It comes from your own mind, and depends upon your ability to place yourself in the service of others.

❧

Making indiscriminate use of teachings so as to pass judgment on people or situations is not a positive activity. It is the sign of a closing of the heart and mind. A given practice or technique is not necessarily adaptable to all circumstances. Teachings must never be used for self-justification against evidence of your error.

❧

Someone who spends endless hours in meditation, yet is not concerned with helping others, and does not manifest generosity and selflessness, is not engaged in effective practice.

❧

The meditative mind does not dwell in some vague, misty realm which is out of touch with reality. Nothingness is not a Buddhist concept. What the concept of emptiness teaches is not non-existence, but the intrinsic non-existence of all phenomena. To accept and understand that nothing has any existence in itself does not lead to nihilism.

❧

The first step in spiritual practice is vigilance regarding the production of negative thoughts and words.

❧

Change is always possible. We only have to desire it and act accordingly. We are all capable of this.

❧

Ordeals reveal whether a disciple is a real practitioner. The true nature of a person becomes outwardly manifest in such moments.

❧

True effort means rejoicing in one's freedom to act in a positive and constructive manner.

❧

Western psychology endeavors to dissolve emotional problems at their source. But since it rejects any principle involving the concept of rebirth, it accords too large a place to unconsciousness. The notion of rebirth is essential for insight into the mechanisms at work in important life-situations.

❧

Inner transformation is a long-term affair. Patience enables one to accept the slowness of this process.

❧

It is good to devote special time every evening to recollection of all the thoughts and actions which have shaped who we have been during that day. If what we have been doing is in accord with our spiritual commitment, it is good to rejoice. And if the contrary is the case, it is good to feel a regret which will help us to prevent repeating actions in disharmony with the values of our practice.

❧

The practices taught in Buddhism enable us to climb major passes. Once these thresholds are crossed, negative emotions only have minor effects upon us. Like the foam of a wave, which has no real impact upon the ocean itself, such emotions now become the signs of the end of a movement.

❧

A prostration before an image of the Buddha or before a master is not an homage to a god or other divine figure. It is instead an expression of our recognition of our fundamental nature: total, absolute, luminous knowledge of reality, free of all ignorance.

❧

Buddhas have made a vow to liberate beings from this illusory cycle of the reign of suffering. Their actions are manifested through human masters, who are their supports and channels. Masters open doors which give us access to the different actions of these Buddhas. The reason we regard masters symbolically as real Buddhas is so that the latter can act through them.

❧

Initiations have now become fashionable. But if you do not engage in practice, you cannot receive the true essence of an initiation. You will probably have a good experience, but it will have no effect upon your evolution.

❧

As soon as you wake up in the morning, bring your motivation into sharp focus and resolve to live your life in a positive way.

❧

If you engage in sincere practice for several years, you cannot fail to observe that changes are taking place in you.

❧

Learning mastery of the mind consists of transforming our old mental habits so as to acquire new ones which bring us happiness.

❧

The mind is like a crystal which reflects what is inside us. It adapts itself to what we are.

❧

Consciousness is modulated by the power of our habits. They have a profound effect on the subtle levels of our being. Recognizing them is not enough to dissolve them. Transformation of them also requires will, determination, analysis, reflection, knowledge of the mechanisms at work, and a meditation practice which disciplines the mind.

❧

Liberation from all attachment does not mean becoming indifferent toward others.

❧

True discipline is not imposed. It is based on an understanding and analysis of the phenomena in question. This movement of discipline comes from within, and radiates without.

❧

Meditation shows us how to find the inner peace which flows from a still mind.

❧

Awakening is beyond all concepts. This is why nirvana and awakening cannot be taught. The Buddhist path only shows the skillful means of realizing them.

❧

The path begins with the work of self-transformation. Only then can the possibility of helping others follow.

EPILOGUE: TIBET

It would be unthinkable to overlook the subject of Tibet in any collection of the Dalai Lama's sayings. He is inseparably linked to his country. It is these landscapes and their flora, fauna, and human beings which have shaped the Dalai Lama and his wisdom: a land of contrasts, with a beauty which can be sweet, harsh, magical, or wild and disturbing. It is a land which has a powerful and unforeseeable impact upon those who visit it for the first time. Its density vibrates in his very cells. Tibet and the Dalai Lama are not merely two sides of the same coin, they are a Unity. Like a precious jewel, he reflects the many facets of that other jewel, his country of origin. To understand something about Tibet is to understand something about this exceptional being.

Until its annexation by China in 1959, Tibet was basically a feudal society. For many centuries, the Roof of the World had remained beyond the bounds of the rest of the world, isolated by its exceptional geography. Its altitude, its sublime and austere landscapes, limitless spaces, and its culture, religion, and spirituality all contributed to make it an inviolate sanctuary.

During the course of its history, Mongolia, China, and Nepal had invaded the country at different times—sometimes making it into a more or less friendly protectorate—but never with any lasting success. India exercised a different, and crucial influence upon Tibet when Buddhism was introduced there in a decisive manner by Padmasambhava, revered by Tibetans as a second Buddha.

Relations with China were always complex and subtle, but had never been one of total conquest and annexation of one people by another. At one time the Dalai Lama was the spiritual guide of the Chinese emperor, exchanging a spiritual protection on one side for a military protection on the other. But beginning in 1910, the Chinese progressively attempted to distort the history of these bonds in a colonialist propaganda which denies the truth that the two have always been separate and independent countries, geographically, culturally, and politically.

Some important dates of modern Tibetan history:

End of 1949: Invasion of Tibet by the People's Liberation Army of China. During the occupation, Mao promises Tibetan autonomy. The beginning of the total destruction of the historical entity of Tibet.

1951: The Seventeen Point Agreement joins Tibet to its giant neighbor. Several provinces are occupied by Chinese forces, and Tibetan autonomy is reduced by half, in violation of the treaty.

1959: The uprising of March 10th, which marks a pivotal defeat for the Tibetan people. The Dalai Lama is forced to flee to India at the last minute. Over 100,000 Tibetans follow him into exile.

1966–76: The Cultural Revolution in China, a period of extremism which also began its genocidal policy against Tibetan people and culture. Thousands of temples and monasteries are pillaged and destroyed, women are forced to have abortions and sterilizations, sometimes en masse. Chinese is declared as the first language of the country and the language of its schools. It is forbidden to practice Buddhism. And the very land itself is attacked: huge deforestation projects are undertaken, so that the Roof of the World may serve as a strategic site for missiles and other military installations. This also is the beginning of the pollution of Tibet's rivers, which are the source of some of the greatest rivers of Asia.

1965: The first riots in Lhassa.

1988: The Chinese government breaks off all dialogue with Tibetan representatives.

1989: Institution of martial law in Tibet, lasting until 1990. The Nobel Peace Prize is awarded to the Dalai Lama.

1999: Demographic changes reflect the increasing Chinese colonization of Tibet. Now the majority of people in all the largest cities are Chinese. The country contains six million Tibetans and over seven million Chinese.

2000: On January 1st, the seventeenth Karmapa escapes across the border between China and India. He joins the Dalai Lama at Dharamsala. This exile has great significance: until then, the Chinese had two of the three most important dignitaries in Tibetan Buddhism in their power: the Panchen Lama, and the Karmapa. They were waiting for the present Dalai Lama to die, hoping to then gain control of the religion itself, by "discovering" their own fifteenth Dalai Lama. This would have given them an enormous and demoralizing power over Tibetans, especially inside Tibet, perhaps ultimately breaking their very faith itself. The young Panchen

Lama officially recognized by the present Dalai Lama, was rejected by the Chinese and imprisoned. They then replaced him with another Panchen Lama of their choice. At this date, the true Panchen Lama is the world's youngest political prisoner.

This meeting in a free country between the fourteenth Dalai Lama and the young seventeenth Karmapa was a powerful and significant event, especially for the survival of Tibetan culture and religion. This is why reports of intensifying Chinese repression against lamas began to come out of Tibet afterwards.

At the date of this writing, human rights are practically nonexistent in Tibet. The international community has not offered a great deal of support, at least on the governmental level.

However, the World Bank has for the first time refused funds intended for China, because they were to be used to finance more emigration of Chinese settlers into Tibet. But in general, Western authorities seem indifferent to the fate of Tibet. The Dalai Lama was recently denied permission to participate in the Millennium Summit in New York, where he, along with all the world's greatest religious leaders, had been invited. This shocking and cowardly decision of course shows the pressure that the Peking regime is able to bring to bear on the worlds greatest powers.

Roof of the World

Truth, courage, determination, justice, and non-violence: these are the only arms in our battle to regain our freedom of action and of thought in Tibet.

❧

Never forget that we are exiles, and that someday this exile will end.

❧

Exile has forced us to transform some of the ancient cultural and ancestral traditions which formed our civilization. But the cultural foundations arising from spiritual knowledge have been preserved. Whatever country we find ourselves in, we must continue to express our traditional values of courage, tolerance, non-violence, compassion, and respect for nature and for animals. These values are our roots. We have transmitted them from generation to generation since time immemorial.

❧

My dearest wish is to see Tibet someday become a land of refuge for human beings and animals. A sanctuary of peace and freedom where people can come for refreshment of the soul, discovering in themselves the calm, peace, serenity, and happiness that are so often lacking in Western societies.

A free Tibet will be a democracy in itself. We will preserve our cultural identity and religion, and we will add to these a further richness of knowledge which we have acquired from our contact with modern civilization while in exile.

As long as Tibet is not free, as long as my people need me as the Dalai Lama, I will continue to be reborn—outside my native country—so as to fulfill this role. The purpose of each of these rebirths is to continue work begun in the previous life, work which was incomplete at the time of death. As the fourteenth Dalai Lama, my task is to do my utmost so that my people can return home, to a country which is free and autonomous. This work I intend to complete, even if it means I have to die and be reborn many more times.

When Tibet finally becomes free and autonomous, I will abandon all of my official and political activities. I will become a simple monk, close to my people—and more available and useful to them as well.

Forgiveness

The situation in Tibet is especially dire and dramatic. Yet I feel no animosity, no hate, nor any other aggressive emotion toward the Chinese people. My duty is to serve all human beings. If the Chinese ever need me, I will help them.

❧

Tibet was a completely independent country for centuries, but it would be utopian to hope for the return of this kind of status now.

❧

The Tibetan cause is a just one. I believe that we will some-day return to our country. The world situation and human consciences are evolving. This is why it would be a mistake to isolate China diplomatically and economically. China is a very powerful nation, and it has an interest in living in har-mony with the West and with its own neighbors. Its people desire freedom of action and thought, just as other people do. Changes are already happening there. Most of them are invisible, but they have begun.

❧

Books by His Holiness the Dalai Lama and Other Buddhist Titles

Beyond Dogma: Dialogues and Discourses
By His Holiness the Dalai Lama
$14.95 trade paper, 244 pp.
ISBN: 1-55643-218-6

Beyond Dogma presents a record of a 1993 visit to France by His Holiness the Dalai Lama, recipient of the 1989 Nobel Peace Prize. During a series of public lectures and question-and-answer sessions with political activists, religious leaders, students, scientists, Buddhist practitioners, and interfaith organizations, His Holiness responds to a wide range of topics, including: the practice of Buddhism in the West; nonviolence, human rights, and the Tibetan crisis; ecumenical approaches to spirituality; the meeting of Buddhism and science; and more.

Essential Teachings
By His Holiness the Dalai Lama
Introduction by Andrew Harvey
$14.95 trade paper, 152 pp.
ISBN: 1-55643-192-9

"This book is Buddhism purified to its simplest human essence, an essence that transcends all barriers, all colors and creeds. It is a philosophy of the most urgent, practical, active altruism constructed not in a study but lived out at the center of a storm of violence."
—from the Introduction by Andrew Harvey, *Return of the Mother* and *The Way of Passion: A Celebration*

**Blossoms of the Dharma:
Living as a Buddhist Nun**
By Thubten Chodron
Foreword by Sylvia Boorstein
$16.95 trade paper, 242 pp.
b&w photos
ISBN: 1-55643-325-5

This book gathers some of the presentations and teachings from a 1996 conference in Dharamsala, India, on "Life as a Western Buddhist Nun." His Holiness the Dalai Lama supported the effort of Buddhist nuns to clarify their purpose in taking vows, widening their context, broadening community beyond their own abbeys, and achieving greater equality with men in liturgical matters, especially ordination.

**Buddhist Women on the Edge:
Contemporary Perspectives from the
Western Frontier**
Edited by Marianne Dresser
$16.95 trade paper, 338 pp.
ISBN: 1-55643-203-8

Explore this landmark anthology that covers a wide range of issues around gender, race, class, and sexuality in Buddhism. Contributors include Anne Klein, bell hooks, Miranda Shaw, Tsultrim Allione, Shosan Victoria Austin, and others. These essays range across issues of lineage and authority; monastic, lay, and community practice; the teacher-student relationship; psychological perspectives; and the ro! of emotions.

Tenzin Gyatso:
The Early Life of the Dalai Lama
By Claude Levenson
Translated by Joseph Rowe
$14.95 trade paper, 200 pp.
ISBN: 1-55643-383-2

Tenzin Gyatso focuses on the formative years of the fourteenth Dalai Lama, before he became a worldwide presence and peace activist. It is the authoritative biography of the first twenty-four years of his life as told by a close personal friend and prolific journalist, Claude B. Levenson. This biography follows the long and arduous path that the Dalai Lama traveled from his birth in 1935 to his exile to India at the age of twenty-four.

The Tibetan Book of the Dead for Reading Aloud
Adapted by Jean-Claude van Itallie
$20.00 trade paper, 78 pp.
color photos and drawings
ISBN: 1-55643-273-9

Jean-Claude van Itallie's poetic adaptation of traditional Tibetan passages to aid and comfort at the time of death is presented here, accompanied by vivid ...phs, Tibetan art, and other evocative images. The text leads us ...e stages we experience after death and helps us to overcome ...s, desires, jealousies, and fears that can obscure an under-...sitions into the next life.